SABRINA GHAYOUR

BAZAAR

VIBRANT VEGETARIAN RECIPES

MITCHELL BEAZLEY

To my darling boys; my wonderfully funny, intelligent, kind, and crazy nephews Cyrus, Darius, Kasra, and Dastan. Thank you for always being my biggest and most fierce supporters, for each of your unique personalities and differing opinions that have given me much insight into both food and life, as well as your no-nonsense, blunt deliveries if ever I've gone wrong. Love you boys. This one is for you.

An Hachette UK Company
www.hachette.co.uk

First published in Great Britain in 2019 by Mitchell Beazley,
an imprint of Octopus Publishing Group Ltd.
Carmelite House, 50 Victoria Embankment, London EC4Y 0DZ
www.octopusbooks.co.uk

Distributed in the US by Hachette Book Group
1290 Avenue of the Americas, 4th and 5th Floors, New York, NY 10104

Distributed in Canada by Canadian Manda Group
664 Annette St., Toronto, Ontario, Canada M6S 2C8

Text copyright © Sabrina Ghayour 2019
Photography copyright © Kris Kirkham 2019
Design and layout copyright © Octopus Publishing Group Ltd 2019

ISBN 978 1 78472 575 4

A CIP catalog record for this book is available from the British Library.

Printed and bound in China

10 9 8 7 6 5 4 3 2 1

Publishing Director: Stephanie Jackson
Managing Editor: Sybella Stephens
Copy Editor: Salima Hirani
Creative Director: Jonathan Christie
Senior Designer: Jaz Bahra
Illustrator: Abigail Read
Photographer: Kris Kirkham
Food Stylist: Laura Field
Props Stylist: Agathe Gits
Senior Production Manager: Peter Hunt

Note on ingredients
Sea salt flakes should be used where stated (Sabrina cooks with Maldon sea salt flakes).
Always use genuine, alcohol-free rose water.

CONTENTS

INTRODUCTION

"Bazaar" is the ancient Persian word for "market" and is shared by many other Eastern cultures. If I close my eyes, I imagine the old traditional markets of the Middle East in years gone by, which were loud, bustling places filled with colorful produce of every shape and description. Unusual smells would fill the air. The senses would be seduced at every turn as sights and sounds distracted all those coming into the bazaar, luring them to the many stands to fulfill their various requirements. No matter which country I travel to, one of my greatest joys is visiting a good market that retains a focus on fresh and simple produce, untainted by modernity or the bells and whistles of trendy treats. There is always inspiration and a culinary education to be had in every local bazaar. Having long thought of myself as one of the world's most consummate carnivores, I never thought I would see the day when I put pen to paper to write a book of vegetarian recipes. Why, you may ask. Well, simply put, in many cultures, including my own, if there is no meat on the table, the meal is considered incomplete. Some cultures have endured war and famine where food, and especially meat, have been scarce. As times improve, meat often becomes the centerpiece of any feast, as a sign that life is good and you are doing well, which is a tradition still evident in many cultures. I know that whenever I cook a meatless feast for my family, I don't announce it in advance for fear of the unnecessary but hilarious panic it would cause!

Recently, I have noticed that more and more people are choosing to eat less meat. I have found that, as I get older, I simply don't seem able to enjoy meat in the excessive and voracious manner in which I used to, or digest it as easily. Having said that, I remain the world's safest bet for winner of the "Least Likely To Turn Vegetarian" prize so, for me, this is a book that showcases and celebrates how wonderful and satisfying meals can be when they contain only fruits, vegetables, legumes, grains, and dairy products. This is something that I myself can occasionally forget.

I have written this book with meat-eaters in mind, because I feel it is we who really need the most help and inspiration when it comes to preparing simple meals without meat, which have plenty of flavor and satisfy all at the table.

I have started teaching many vegetarian cooking classes lately and have noticed that the vast majority of my students are not actually vegetarians, but rather those who eat meat and fish. They come in search of ideas to help them deliver delicious meals at home without falling back on the same old repertoire. I love taking time off from eating meat, but have often been guilty of resorting to the usual suspects for sustenance. And while pasta, potatoes, bread, rice, and mountains of cheese have their advantages and frequently satisfy, eventually you do just crave vegetables. Their colors, freshness, depth of flavors, and varied textures sustain the desire to stick to a meatless meal. I'm hoping this book provides inspiration to all those who need it, vegetarians and meat-eaters alike.

I created these recipes with a single aim: to deliver as much flavor as possible using few ingredients. The one thing I would like you to remember is that each recipe is merely a suggestion of ingredients. Feel free to add whatever additions you like. Don't stress about ingredients you cannot find. If you are missing an ingredient or don't like something, just omit it because, after all, life is too short to sweat the small stuff. I hope you will embrace these recipes and make them your own. Food should always be a pleasure. My stomach (and my waistline) took great pleasure in perfecting these recipes for you, so take this book into your kitchen and enjoy.

Sabrina Ghayour

LIGHT BITES & SHARING PLATES

CARROT, HALLOUMI & DILL BALLS

Rarely do you see carrots fried, so here I've combined them with halloumi to make these crispy little balls. Perfect with drinks or as part of a feast, this is probably one of the best things that ever happened to the humble carrot, if I'm honest.

vegetable oil, for frying

2 large carrots, peeled and
    coarsely grated

9oz halloumi cheese, coarsely grated

1 large egg

1 small pack (about 1oz) of dill,
    finely chopped

¼ cup all-purpose flour

2 teaspoons cumin seeds

1 teaspoon paprika

Maldon sea salt flakes and freshly
    ground black pepper

salad greens, to serve

MAKES 16 TO 18

Pour enough vegetable oil into a large saucepan to fill it to a depth of 2 inches. Heat the oil over medium-high heat and bring to frying temperature (add a pinch of the mixture; if it sizzles immediately, the oil is hot enough). Line a plate with a double layer of paper towels.

Add the grated carrot and halloumi, along with the remaining ingredients, to a mixing bowl and season well with black pepper and just a little salt. Now work the mixture with your hands to combine it well.

When the oil is ready for deep-frying, take roughly 1 tablespoon of the mixture and roll it into a ball that would fit perfectly into the tablespoon measure. Repeat with the remaining mixture. Carefully lower the balls into the hot oil and fry in batches for 2 to 3 minutes, until deep golden brown. Remove with a slotted spoon and transfer to the prepared plate to drain. Serve hot with salad greens.

FAVA BEAN & RICOTTA DIP

Fava beans carry so many childhood memories for me. Arriving home from school on the rare occasion my Grandma was making one of the handful of dishes she learned to make in the 1980s, she would sit me down in front of enormous bowls of fava beans with skins on. All she would say was, "Peel them." I remember the overpowering smell of the skins on my hands when we were done peeling, but it was worth the effort because the beans were so delicious. This serves recipe is perfect for sharing.

approximately 1¾lb frozen (skin-on) or 2¾ cups peeled fava beans

2 fat garlic cloves, crushed

finely grated zest and juice of 1 unwaxed lemon

good drizzle of olive oil, plus a little extra to serve

16oz ricotta cheese

2 teaspoons sumac

4 scallions, very thinly sliced from root to tip

1 small pack (about 1oz) of dill, finely chopped

Maldon sea salt flakes and freshly ground black pepper

toasted bread, to serve

SERVES 6 TO 8

If using frozen skin-on fava beans, rinse them to remove any ice, then cook in boiling water for 5 minutes. Drain the beans in a sieve and rinse under cold running water to stop the cooking process. Keep rinsing them until cool enough to handle.

Peel each bean to remove the outer skin and place the peeled beans in the bowl of a food processor. Add the garlic, lemon zest and juice, and olive oil to the bowl and pulse to grind down the mixture to a nice chunky texture, ensuring no large chunks remain.

Transfer the mixture to a large serving bowl. Add the ricotta, sumac, scallions, dill, plenty of freshly milled black pepper, and a good amount of salt. Mix well, then let stand for 5 to 10 minutes to allow the flavors to develop. Adjust the seasoning if necessary, then drizzle with extra olive oil and serve with toasted bread.

SUMAC, TOMATO & GARLIC ON TOAST
WITH LABNEH

I'm obsessed with tomatoes on toast either in the Spanish style of pan con tomate or the Italian bruschetta. I used to make mini versions of these for clients as canapés, which proved so popular that I was asked to serve them as appetizers rather than finger food. The addition of sumac gives the tomatoes a citrusy note, and I never need an excuse to add cilantro to tomatoes. These are incredibly delicious and I am happy to eat several of these as a meal by themselves; simple yet terribly good.

1 large ciabatta, cut into 12 slices

1 large or 2 small garlic cloves, peeled

4 large, ripe vine tomatoes,
   very finely chopped

½ small red onion, very finely diced

2 teaspoons sumac, plus extra to garnish

½ small packet (about ½oz) of fresh
   cilantro, finely chopped (reserve
   some for garnish)

olive oil

heaped ¼ cup labneh or thick Greek
   yogurt, divided

Maldon sea salt flakes and freshly
   ground black pepper

MAKES 12

Chargrill the bread on both sides on a ridged grill pan over high heat, or use a toaster. Lightly rub the top surface of each slice with the raw garlic.

Mix the tomatoes, onion, sumac, and cilantro in a bowl. Add a little drizzle of olive oil and season well with salt and pepper.

Divide the tomato mixture between the pieces of toast, spreading it across the surface of each piece. Top each with a teaspoon of labneh or yogurt and garnish each with a little pinch of sumac, the reserved cilantro, and a drizzle of olive oil. Serve immediately.

POTATO SKINS STUFFED WITH FETA & SCALLIONS

Nothing hollers comfort to me more than creamy mashed potatoes, and this dish provides a delicious twist by combining it with another favorite of mine, the humble potato skin. This is simple, delicious, and very filling, and you can easily adapt the flavors to use up whatever other ingredients you have lurking in your fridge. It's also perfect for little hands, and kids just love making these.

4 baking potatoes

¼ cup butter

5 to 6 scallions, thinly sliced from
    root to tip

7oz feta cheese, crumbled

½ small pack (about ½oz) of tarragon,
    leaves finely chopped

1 tablespoon garlic granules

1 teaspoon nigella seeds

Maldon sea salt flakes and freshly
    ground black pepper

SERVES 4 TO 6

Preheat the oven to 425°F.

Place the whole potatoes on a baking pan and bake for 25 to 30 minutes, then reduce the oven temperature to 400°F, and bake for a further 1 hour, until the potatoes are cooked through. Remove from the oven.

Let the potatoes cool slightly, then cut each one in half. Scoop out the flesh from each half into a bowl and set aside the skins.

Season the flesh generously with salt and pepper and add the butter to the bowl. Using a potato masher or a fork, coarsely mash the butter, salt, and pepper into the potato (don't worry if the mixture is not completely smooth). Use a spoon to stir in the scallions, feta, tarragon, garlic granules, and nigella seeds and mix well. Adjust the seasoning if desired.

Fill the potato skins with the mashed mixture, packing the filling in firmly. Set the stuffed skins on a baking pan and bake for 30 minutes, or until just starting to brown on top. Serve hot.

CHICKPEA & VEGETABLE KOFTAS

WITH TAHINI SAUCE

Someone already had the idea of inventing falafel wraps, so I came up with this lighter version, which is absolutely delicious, packs in the vegetables, and can easily be adapted to suit whatever you have in the fridge. With all the appeal of an indulgent kebab, these koftas are equally irresistible on their own with a drizzle of tahini sauce on top.

2 x 14oz cans chickpeas, drained

3 fat garlic cloves, crushed

1 carrot, peeled and grated

1 sweet potato (about 10½oz), grated
    with the skin left on

1 small pack (about 1oz) of fresh cilantro,
    finely chopped (reserve a large pinch
    to serve)

4 scallions, finely sliced

1 teaspoon turmeric

1 teaspoon ground cumin

1 teaspoon ground cinnamon

1 teaspoon dried red chile flakes

¼ cup chickpea (gram) flour

1 egg

generous amount of Maldon sea salt
    flakes and freshly ground black pepper

vegetable oil, for frying

For the tahini sauce

⅔ cup Greek yogurt

1 garlic clove, crushed

2 teaspoons ground coriander

3 tablespoons thick tahini

juice of ½ lemon

To serve

6 tortilla wraps

few handfuls of arugula leaves

1 red onion, halved and thinly sliced

MAKES 18 TO 20

Place the chickpeas into a large mixing bowl and use a potato masher or the end of a rolling pin to mash them. Add all the remaining kofta ingredients, except the oil, and using your hands pummel or pound (which is what the word "kofta" means in Persian) into a sticky, even mixture. Let refrigerate while you make the tahini sauce.

To make the tahini sauce, combine the ingredients in a small bowl, then season with salt and pepper. Add just enough warm water loosen to a thick creamy consistency. Set aside.

Pour enough vegetable oil into a large, deep skillet or saucepan to fill to a depth of about 1 inch. Heat the oil over medium-high heat and bring to frying temperature (add a pinch of the kofta mixture; if it sizzles immediately, the oil is hot enough). Line a large baking pan with a double layer of paper towels.

When the oil is ready for frying, scoop up a rounded tablespoonful of the kofta mixture and use the edges of the bowl to smooth it a little. Lower it carefully into the hot oil. Repeat with the remaining mixture, but do not overcrowd the pan (cook in batches to avoid reducing the temperature of the oil). Fry the koftas for a couple of minutes on each side, or until deep golden brown, then remove them from the pan using a slotted spoon and transfer to the prepared baking pan to drain.

Serve 3 koftas in each tortilla wrap with a generous drizzle of the tahini sauce, some arugula, some sliced red onion, and a final flourish of the reserved cilantro.

SPICED BUTTERMILK FRIED TOMATOES

This is definitely one of my better ideas. When I made my mother try it, with her first bite she smiled and said, "How on earth do you come up with this stuff?" Rest assured, this is her unique way of paying a compliment. My only advice is, don't be tempted to use ripe tomatoes for this recipe. Here, the firmer and more underripe, the better.

vegetable oil, for frying

1⅔ cups best-quality polenta
(not quick-cook)

1 cup buttermilk

1 teaspoon cayenne pepper

2 teaspoons garlic granules

2 teaspoons sumac

4 large tomatoes, such as beefsteak
tomatoes

3 tablespoons dried wild oregano

Maldon sea salt flakes and freshly
ground black pepper

SERVES 4 TO 6

Pour enough vegetable oil into a large, deep skillet or saucepan to fill to a depth of about 1 inch. Heat the oil over medium-high heat and bring to frying temperature (add a little polenta; if it sizzles immediately, the oil is hot enough). Line a plate with a double layer of paper towels.

Pour the polenta onto a plate and set aside. In a separate bowl, mix the buttermilk with the cayenne pepper, garlic granules, sumac, and a generous amount of salt and pepper.

Cut the tomatoes into slices ½ inch thick (I usually get about 4 slices per tomato). Polenta doesn't stick to the skin very easily, so discard the ends.

Drag a tomato slice through the buttermilk and shake off any excess liquid, then place it gently in the polenta and coat the cut sides and the edges as best you can, carefully patting the polenta onto the slice to encrust it. Lower it carefully into the hot oil, then repeat with the remaining tomato slices, frying in batches to avoid overcrowding the pan. Gently fry the slices for about 1 minute on each side, or until they start to brown. If they brown too fast, your oil is too hot, in which case, turn off the heat and cook a few slices. Then, when the oil returns to the right temperature, turn the heat back on.

Remove the slices from the oil with a slotted spoon and transfer to the prepared plate to drain. Sprinkle with some salt and scatter with the oregano. Serve the tomatoes hot.

CUCUMBER & FETA BRUSCHETTA

This is one of my favorite breakfasts. Sounds weird, but I am addicted to the combination of yogurt mixed with feta and topped with cucumber. It really does make the most satisfying snack, and the spices and pomegranate seeds take it to another level. They can also easily be made in smaller bites and served as finger food, too. Use half a regular cucumber thinly sliced into half-moons if you can't find baby cucumbers.

7oz feta cheese, finely crumbled

½ cup Greek yogurt

6 slices of sourdough bread

5 to 6 baby cucumbers, cut diagonally into slices ¼ inch thick

1 teaspoon sumac

1 teaspoon dried wild oregano

1 teaspoon pul biber chile flakes

½ teaspoon nigella seeds

¼ cup pomegranate seeds

olive oil, for drizzling (optional)

Maldon sea salt flakes and freshly ground black pepper

SERVES 6

Combine the feta and yogurt in a bowl. Mash the mixture with a fork to combine. Season with black pepper and just a little salt.

Chargrill the sourdough on both sides in a ridged grill pan placed on medium-high heat or use a toaster.

Divide the feta mixture into 6 portions and spread a portion onto each slice of toast. Arrange the cucumber slices on top, then sprinkle with the sumac, oregano, and pul biber.

Scatter with the nigella seeds and, lastly, the pomegranate seeds. Drizzle with a little olive oil, if desired, and serve immediately.

TURMERIC, SPINACH & SWEET POTATO FRITTERS

There are very few things that aren't improved by frying and that includes vegetables, especially sweet potatoes. Turmeric is underrated as a spice, but I like it to be a main player in my cooking, just so long as it is not too overpowering and strikes the perfect balance with the other ingredients in a recipe. Eat these fritters with a few dipping sauces on the side—sweet chili sauce is my personal favorite pairing.

10½oz sweet potato, peeled and
    coarsely grated

5½oz baby spinach, finely chopped

1 tablespoon turmeric

1 teaspoon dried red chile flakes

3 large eggs

¾ cup all-purpose flour

1 teaspoon baking powder

vegetable oil, for frying

Maldon sea salt flakes and freshly ground
    black pepper

sweet chili sauce, to serve

MAKES APPROXIMATELY 20

Add the sweet potato, spinach, turmeric, red chile flakes, eggs, flour, and baking powder to a mixing bowl and stir to combine. Season generously with salt and pepper, then let the batter rest for 15 minutes.

Pour enough vegetable oil into a large, deep skillet or saucepan to fill to a depth of about 2 inches. Heat the oil over medium-high heat and bring to frying temperature (add a little of the batter; if it sizzles immediately, the oil is hot enough). Line a plate with a double layer of paper towels.

When the oil is ready, stir the batter well. Using 2 tablespoons, form quenelles of the mixture: scoop up the mixture with one spoon and use the other to press down and shape it. Lower the quenelles carefully into the hot oil and fry in batches, 6 at a time. It is important not to overcrowd the pan or the temperature of the oil will drop and your fritters will not be crisp. Fry the fritters for 1 minute, then turn them over and fry for another minute or so, or until nicely browned all over. Remove the fritters from the oil using a slotted spoon and transfer to the prepared plate to drain. Serve hot with sweet chili sauce.

SPICED CRUDITÉ PLATTER

WITH TURMERIC & CUMIN HUMMUS

Sometimes we all need a little encouragement when it comes to consuming raw vegetables, though Persians like to snack on large quantities of seasoned baby cucumbers. The simple spice treatment on this crudité platter transforms humble raw vegetables into something special, particularly when served with my chunky turmeric and cumin hummus. This highly flavorsome spice blend takes raw vegetables to the next level with minimum effort and maximum effect. It's easy to eat half this platter in no time at all.

1 large cucumber, cut into batons

5½oz radishes, halved

4 to 5 celery stalks (with leaves), cut into 2-inch batons

9oz cherry or baby plum tomatoes

8 carrots, peeled and halved lengthwise (or 4 large carrots, peeled and cut into batons)

olive oil, for drizzling

Maldon sea salt flakes and freshly ground black pepper

For the toasted-spice seasoning

1 teaspoon cumin seeds

1 teaspoon coriander seeds

1 teaspoon yellow mustard seeds

½ teaspoon dried red chile flakes

1 teaspoon dried wild oregano

For the turmeric & cumin hummus

2 x 14oz cans chickpeas (reserve the liquid from 1 can, drain the second can)

½oz piece fresh turmeric, peeled and finely grated

1 fat garlic clove, minced

2 teaspoons cumin seeds, toasted and crushed using a mortar and pestle

finely grated zest and juice of 1 unwaxed lemon

4 teaspoons tahini

olive oil, for drizzling

SERVES 6 TO 8

To make the toasted-spice seasoning, heat a small skillet over medium heat. Add the cumin, coriander seeds, and mustard seeds to the dry pan and toast them, shaking the pan, for 2 minutes. Transfer the toasted seeds to a mortar and pestle, then mix in the red chile flakes and grind to a coarse powder. Stir in the oregano, then set aside.

To make the turmeric and cumin hummus, use a food processor or blender to blitz 1 can of chickpeas, including the canning liquid, until completely smooth. Add a generous amount of salt and pepper, the fresh turmeric, garlic, crushed cumin seeds, lemon zest and juice, and tahini. Blitz again briefly until the ingredients are all well incorporated.

Add the remaining can of drained chickpeas and pulse briefly to break them down slightly. I like a nice chunky texture, but if you prefer a smooth hummus, continue to blitz until the mixture is smooth. Check and adjust the seasoning, adding salt and pepper as necessary. Transfer the hummus to a serving bowl and drizzle with some olive oil.

Arrange the prepared vegetables attractively on a serving platter (place the cucumber batons skin-side down). Drizzle with a good amount of olive oil, season generously with salt and pepper, then season heavily with the toasted-spice seasoning. Serve immediately with the hummus served on the side for dipping.

POTATO CHIPS
WITH SPICED SALT & LIME

I have a life-long obsession with potato chips. Over the years I have become something of a self-styled potato chip aficionado, pairing them with different cheeses and cured meats (because that's all I have the energy to eat after a 17-hour shift cooking food for others). So I like to think I'm now a bit of a connoisseur. This is a spectacular treatment for the humble chip, but to be perfectly honest, you can use a store-bought bag of good-quality, hand-cooked plain potato chips. However, nothing beats the flavor of homemade potato chips, so these are very much worth the effort.

4 potatoes (unpeeled)

1 tablespoon fine sea salt

about 1 quart vegetable or sunflower oil, for deep-frying

2 limes, cut into wedges, to serve

For the spiced salt

2 tablespoons Maldon sea salt flakes or 1 tablespoon fine salt

½ teaspoon chili powder

½ teaspoon ground coriander

½ teaspoon dried wild oregano

½ teaspoon sumac

SERVES 6 TO 8

Using a mandoline or a food processor slicing attachment set to medium thickness, thinly slice the potatoes to the thickness of a matchstick. Alternatively, thinly slice them by hand. Rinse the slices to remove any excess starch, then let them soak for about 20 minutes in a large mixing bowl filled with cold water and the fine sea salt.

Meanwhile, using a mortar and pestle, grind the spiced salt ingredients together. Set aside.

Once the soaking time has elapsed, drain the potato slices, rinse them, then dry them as well as you can with a clean dishcloth or paper towels.

Pour enough vegetable or sunflower oil into a large, deep skillet or saucepan to fill to a depth of about 2½ inches. Alternatively heat a deep-fat fryer. Heat the oil over medium-high heat and bring to frying temperature (add a slice of potato; if it sizzles immediately, the oil is hot enough). Line a large baking pan with a double layer of paper towels.

You'll need to fry the potato slices in batches, depending on the size of your pan. Carefully lower the first batch of potato slices into the hot oil stir gently with a slotted spoon to stop them sticking together, and fry for a few minutes, or until golden brown. Remove the cooked chips from the hot oil using a slotted spoon and transfer to the prepared plate to drain. Repeat with the remaining batches of potato slices.

To serve, place the chips on a board or flat platter and season with the spiced salt as desired. Serve with the lime wedges. Squeeze some lime juice onto the chips just before eating.

TURMERIC, LEMON & VODKA COOLERS

Herbs, aromatics, spices, and even vegetables can provide a base for some interesting tipples. If there is a cocktail with turmeric in it on a bar menu, it's virtually a given that I will be ordering it. My love for turmeric runs so deep that I came up with this blend inspired by the hot drink I make when I need a natural remedy to fight a cold. Although I must admit, I much prefer this medicine in cocktail form!

ice cubes or crushed ice

10½ to 14fl oz vodka
   (use 1½fl oz per cocktail)

lemon slices, to garnish (optional)

For the turmeric syrup

3 cups boiling water

1 unwaxed lemon, rind peeled into strips,
   plus the juice

1oz piece fresh turmeric, peeled and cut
   into coarse chunks

¾ cup superfine sugar

MAKES 6 TO 8

First make the syrup. Heat a small saucepan over low heat. Pour in the measured boiling water, then add the strips of lemon rind, the lemon juice, turmeric chunks, and the sugar. Stir briefly until the sugar dissolves. Let the mixture cook very gently. Do not let it simmer or bubble to avoid any liquid evaporating. After 20 minutes, remove the pan from the heat, stir the contents, then let cool completely.

Fill a highball glass two-thirds full with ice cubes or crushed ice and add ½ cup of the cooled turmeric syrup, followed by 1½fl oz vodka. Stir, then add more ice, garnish with a lemon slice, if desired, and serve immediately. Repeat with the remaining turmeric syrup and vodka.

Top left: Barberry Martinis;

Top right: Ginger, Honey & Lime Margaritas

Center: Turmeric, Lemon & Vodka Coolers

GINGER, HONEY & LIME MARGARITAS

Tequila gets such a bad rap, perhaps because many of us have some sort of tequila story that didn't end well. I have a love for good tequila, and classic Margaritas are a favorite of mine. I love lime in pretty much every cocktail, but it's the ginger and honey that make this drink so spectacular. Therefore, this recipe comes with a warning: you may find yourself making many of these. They are just too good!

1½fl oz white tequila

juice of 1 lime

1-inch piece of fresh ginger root,
    peeled and grated

1 tablespoon liquid honey

ice cubes

MAKES 1

Pour the tequila into a tumbler (or cocktail shaker), add the lime juice, ginger, and honey and stir the mixture well to ensure the honey dissolves. Once the honey has dissolved, add ice and stir using a chopstick or similar (or shake if using a cocktail shaker) until chilled, then strain the drink into a Margarita glass and serve.

BARBERRY MARTINIS

Some would argue that drinks are every bit as important as the food at a good meal. I must confess that I have never placed great importance on liquid refreshment, instead always throwing myself into producing really good food. But for me, a good cocktail relies on a few factors: sweet, sour, cold, and refreshing. This barberry Martini (or Bar-tini!) does the job beautifully.

2 cups boiling water

⅔ cup dried barberries

¼ cup honey

7fl oz vodka

8 to 10 ice cubes

MAKES 8

Pour the measured boiling water over the barberries and let infuse until the liquid has cooled completely. Blitz the mixture in a high powered blender until completely smooth. Strain the liquid into a small pitcher, then add honey and stir until dissolved.

Add the vodka, which should take the volume of liquid to approximately 3½ cups. Pour half this mixture into a cocktail shaker, add half the ice cubes, and shake until cold. Strain into 4 Martini glasses. Repeat with remaining mixture and ice cubes.

EGGS & DAIRY

GRILLED HALLOUMI FLATBREADS

WITH PRESERVED LEMON & BARBERRY SALSA

This is my version of a taco, but with all the punch and vibrancy you would associate with Middle Eastern flavors. You can also use Indian paneer or tofu instead of halloumi. The flatbreads alone are so incredibly delicious you may never buy store-bought flatbreads again.

2 x 9oz blocks halloumi cheese

2 tablespoons Greek-style yogurt

2-inch piece of fresh turmeric, peeled and finely grated

1 garlic clove, crushed

finely grated zest of 1 unwaxed lime

good squeeze of lime juice

vegetable oil

1 x recipe "Shaken" Sweet Quick Pickled Onions (*see page 193*)

pul biber chile flakes, to garnish

Maldon sea salt flakes and black pepper

For the flatbreads

2 tablespoons unsalted butter, melted

1½ cups all-purpose flour

½ cup lowfat milk

2 teaspoons freshly ground black pepper

2 teaspoons garlic granules

1 tablespoon olive oil

For the salsa

½ small pack (about ½oz) of fresh dill, coarsely chopped

4 preserved lemons, seeded and very finely chopped

1 tablespoon dried barberries

1 avocado, peeled, stoned, and coarsely diced

2 teaspoons nigella seeds

For the harissa yogurt

1 cup Greek-style yogurt

1 heaped tablespoon rose harissa

MAKES 4

Cut each block of halloumi into 4 thick equal slices. Put the yogurt, grated turmeric, crushed garlic, and lime zest into a bowl, add the lime juice, and mix well. Season with salt and pepper. Let the halloumi slices marinate while you're making the flatbreads.

Put all the flatbread ingredients, except the oil, into a mixing bowl and mix until a firm dough has formed. Seal the dough in plastic wrap and let rest at room temperature for 30 minutes.

To make the salsa, mix the ingredients together in a small bowl, season with salt and pepper, and set aside.

To make the harissa yoghurt, mix the ingredients together in another bowl, season with salt and pepper, and chill until ready to serve.

When you're ready to cook the flatbreads, preheat a large skillet over medium heat. Divide the dough into 4 equal portions and roll out each piece into a thin disk, about 10 inches in diameter. Brush the hot pan with olive oil and cook the flatbreads, one at a time, for about 45 to 60 seconds on each side, or until lightly browned.

In the same pan, heat a drizzle of vegetable oil over medium-high heat. Add the marinated halloumi slices and fry for about 1 minute on each side, or until nicely browned.

Divide the halloumi between the flatbreads and add a generous dollop of the harissa yogurt on top. Add the salsa and some pickled onions, then sprinkle with some pul biber. Roll up and serve immediately.

BAKED HALLOUMI

I cannot exist without halloumi in my refrigerator at all times, and for good reason: it can make a meal in minutes. The more of it I eat, the more of it I crave, so I like to come up with different ways of using it. I think I've cracked it with this spicy, salty, and sweet combo. It's ridiculously simple to make and perfect for tearing into with friends (or, if you are greedy like me, eating alone).

9oz block of halloumi cheese

2 tablespoons rose harissa

2 tablespoons honey

juice of ½ lime

bread, to serve

SERVES 1 TO 4

Preheat the oven to 425°F.

Take a large square of aluminum foil and line it with nonstick parchment paper. Place the block of halloumi onto the center of this double layer.

Mix the harissa, honey, and lime juice together in a small bowl. Pour the mixture over the halloumi. Draw up the parchment paper around and over the block, then repeat with the foil to seal the parcel tightly at the top. Place on a baking pan and bake for 30 minutes, then serve immediately with bread.

SPICED BEAN SCOTCH EGGS

*Scotch eggs are a thing of beauty and are equally good eaten hot or cold. I felt compelled
to come up with a version that packs in plenty of flavor but without the meat. All you need to decide
is whether you prefer a soft, oozy yolk or a hard-boiled egg center.*

2 x 14oz cans kidney beans, drained
   and rinsed

2 teaspoons turmeric

2 teaspoons ground ginger

2 teaspoons ground cinnamon

2 teaspoons pul biber chile flakes

2 carrots, peeled and coarsely grated

1 onion, grated (drain and discard
   the juice)

1 small pack (about ½oz) of dill,
   very finely chopped

8 eggs

2 tablespoons all-purpose flour,
   for dusting

1 to 1¼ cups fine white bread crumbs

vegetable oil, for frying

Maldon sea salt flakes and freshly
   ground black pepper

MAKES 6

Put the beans and spices into a large mixing bowl, add a generous amount of salt and pepper, and mash until the mixture is as smooth as possible. Add the carrot, onion, and dill and mix well using your hands. Refrigerate the mixture until needed.

Place a saucepan half-filled with water over medium-high heat and bring to a boil. Once the water is boiling, carefully lower in 6 of the eggs and boil for 5 minutes if you like them soft-boiled, or 7 minutes for hard-boiled. Drain the eggs and place them under cold running water to stop the cooking process. Once cooled, carefully tap all around the eggshells with a teaspoon and gently peel off the shell, taking care not to break the egg.

Put the flour and bread crumbs into separate bowls. Crack the remaining 2 eggs into a shallow bowl and beat together. Remove the bean mixture from the refrigerator and divide it into 6 equal portions (I weigh the mixture to help divide it equally). Flatten one portion into a patty shape. Gently dust the exterior of an egg with flour, then place it into the center of the bean-mixture patty. Close up the mixture around the egg until it is sealed and smooth. Roll the coated egg first in beaten egg, then in the bread crumbs, taking time to pat them well into the bean mixture. Repeat with the remaining eggs and portions of bean mixture. Freeze the eggs for about 20 minutes, which helps them retain their shape during frying.

Pour enough vegetable oil into a large, deep skillet or saucepan to fill to a depth of about 2¾ inches, or alternatively heat a deep-fat fryer. Heat the oil over medium-high heat and bring to frying temperature (add a pinch of the bread-crumb mixture; if it sizzles immediately, the oil is hot enough). Line a plate with a double layer of paper towels. When the oil is hot, remove the eggs from the freezer. Cook the eggs 2 at a time in the hot oil for 2 to 3 minutes, or until deeply golden brown all over. Remove the eggs from the oil with a slotted spoon and transfer them to the prepared plate to drain. Sprinkle with some salt flakes and serve warm.

EGGPLANT & CARAMELIZED ONION KUKU

Iranians are big fans of kuku, which is essentially a frittata. We have four classic versions, and one of them uses eggplants. Naturally, I have added my own twist in the form of caramelized onions and a little parsley. If you want to make this more of a meal, add feta cheese and serve it with bread.

generous pinch of best-quality saffron threads, ground to a powder using a mortar and pestle

3 tablespoons boiling water

vegetable oil, for frying

4 large eggplants, cut into 1-inch cubes

3 large onions, halved and thinly sliced into half-moons

10 large eggs

2 tablespoons thick Greek yogurt

2 tablespoons all-purpose flour

2 teaspoons baking powder

1 small pack (about 1oz) of flat-leaf parsley, finely chopped

Maldon sea salt flakes and freshly ground black pepper

SERVES 10

Put the saffron powder into a small cup and pour the boiling water over it. Let steep until the liquid is cool.

Line 2 baking pans with a double layer of paper towels. Pour enough vegetable oil into a large saucepan to fill to a depth of about 1 inch. Heat the oil over medium-high heat, then add half the eggplant cubes. Fry for a few minutes, without stirring, until brown and cooked through. (Remove a piece and mash it with a fork; there should be no resistance.) Using a slotted spoon, transfer the eggplant from the pan to one of the prepared baking pans to drain. Place a layer of paper towel on top of the eggplant cubes to absorb the excess oil. Repeat the process with the remaining eggplant cups, adding oil to the pan as necessary. Set the cooked eggplant cubes aside and let cool.

Place another large saucepan over medium heat and drizzle in enough oil to coat the bottom of the pan. Once hot, add the onion and cook for 30 minutes or so, stirring regularly, until soft and cooked through but without blackening. This process requires a little patience, but the flavor will be worthwhile. Remove the onion from the pan using a slotted spoon and transfer to the other prepared baking pan to drain. Let cool.

Preheat the oven to 400°F. Select a large baking pan or ovenproof dish, about 10½ x 8 inches and line it with nonstick parchment paper.

Crack the eggs into a large mixing bowl and beat. Add the saffron solution, yogurt, flour, and baking powder and mix well. Stir in the cooled onion and eggplant along with the parsley, then season generously with salt and pepper and mix well. Pour the mixture into the prepared baking pan or dish and ensure the ingredients are evenly distributed across it. Bake for 30 minutes (check after 25), or until the top is golden and beginning to brown, and a knife inserted into the center comes out clean of raw egg. Let cool slightly, then cut it into slices. Serve with mixed salad greens.

LIME & ALLSPICE PANEER
WITH MANGO CHILE SALSA

What I love about Indian paneer is that it doesn't melt too easily, so is the perfect carrier for marinades and spice rubs. I've turned to allspice—an underused and somewhat misunderstood spice—for this recipe. It was thought to have multiple flavor profiles akin to a blend of many (or "all") spices, which is how it got its name. As a total spice nerd, this sort of trivia fascinates me! The flavor works beautifully with the paneer and the lovely mango salsa.

9oz paneer, cut into 12 equal cubes

For the marinade
finely grated zest of 1 unwaxed lime
1 teaspoon allspice berries, finely ground
    using a mortar and pestle
1 teaspoon garlic granules
2 tablespoons olive oil
1 teaspoon dried wild thyme
generous amount of Maldon sea
    salt flakes

For the mango chile salsa
1 teaspoon black mustard seeds
1 teaspoon coriander seeds
1 ripe mango, peeled, seeded, and
    finely diced
1 long red chile, seeded and very finely
    diced
½ red onion, very finely diced
juice of ½ lime
1 tablespoon olive oil
½ small pack (about ½oz) of fresh
    cilantro, finely chopped
Maldon sea salt flakes and freshly
    ground black pepper

SERVES 2 TO 4

Combine the ingredients for the marinade in a small bowl.

Put the paneer cubes into a food bag and pour in the marinade. Seal the bag, then rub the marinade really well over the cubes to coat them. Set aside for 30 minutes to marinate.

Meanwhile, make the mango chile salsa. Toast the mustard and coriander seeds into a dry skillet over medium heat for 2 minutes, until they release their aroma. Remove from the heat, then crush using a mortar and pestle.

Put the remaining salsa ingredients into a serving bowl, add the crushed seeds, and mix well. Season to taste, then set aside.

Heat a large saucepan over medium heat. Add the paneer, along with the marinade, and fry for about 1 minute on each side, or until nicely browned. Serve immediately, with the mango salsa dotted on top.

POM-BOMBE

I first made this as an alternative to a Christmas cheese board but, quite frankly, it works all year round as a visually spectacular addition to any table. It does require a degree of patience to stud the cheese ball with pomegranate seeds, but it is well worth the effort. This can be made the day before and kept refrigerated until ready to serve. You can also make it as big as you like by doubling or tripling the recipe quantities. Serve it with crispbreads, crackers, toast, and even Belgian endive leaves.

¾ lb soft goat cheese (chèvre with the rind cut off also works)

2 heaped teaspoons sumac

⅓ cup snipped chives

finely grated zest of 1 unwaxed orange

1 to 2 teaspoons pul biber chile flakes

1 cup pomegranate seeds

⅓ cup pistachio nut slivers or ½ cup coarsely chopped whole pistachio nuts

freshly ground black pepper

SERVES 4 TO 6

Mix the cheese, sumac, chives, orange zest, pul biber, and a generous seasoning of pepper in a mixing bowl until evenly combined.

Lay a large sheet of plastic wrap on your work surface. Using a spatula, scrape the cheese mixture out of the bowl and into the center of the plastic wrap. Gather the 4 corners of the plastic wrap together, expel any air, and twist the plastic wrap just above the top of the ball to secure the cheese mixture. Use your hands to form the mixture inside the plastic wrap into a ball. Refrigerate for 30 minutes or, preferably, freeze for about 10 minutes.

Remove the ball from the refrigerator or freezer and peel back the plastic wrap. Place it on a serving plate. Stud the surface of the ball all over with the pomegranate seeds. Scatter the pistachios on top and around the base, studding the ball with a few pieces wherever you can. Cover loosely with plastic wrap and refrigerate until ready to serve.

KALE & CABBAGE KUKU
WITH PINE NUTS

Cabbage is truly underrated. I use cabbage in so many ways, from salads, rice, and pasta to pies, stir-fries, and so much more. This is a delicious take on the most classic of all the Persian kuku (frittata) recipes, and the best news is you can use any type of cabbage or kale you can get your hands on.

vegetable oil

2 red onions, halved and thinly sliced into half-moons

7oz curly kale, tough stalks discarded, finely chopped

7oz cabbage greens, cut into thin ribbons and coarsely chopped

2 teaspoons garlic granules

1 heaped teaspoon ground fenugreek

1 heaped teaspoon turmeric

8 large eggs

2 teaspoons baking powder

2 tablespoons all-purpose flour

2 tablespoons thick Greek yogurt

2 generous handfuls of dried barberries

¼ cup pine nuts

7oz feta cheese, little chunks no larger than ½ inch picked off by hand

Maldon sea salt flakes and freshly ground black pepper

SERVES 4 TO 6

Place a large saucepan over medium heat. Pour in enough vegetable oil to coat the bottom of the pan. Allow it to heat up, then add the onion and fry gently for a few minutes, stirring from time to time, until soft and cooked through.

Increase the heat to medium-high and add the kale. Stir-fry for 2 minutes, or until completely softened and cooked through. Add the cabbage greens and stir-fry for 5 to 6 minutes, then add the garlic granules and spices, season generously with salt and pepper, and mix well. Cook until the cabbage is wilted and cooked through. (You are not aiming to retain the texture or keep the greens al dente for this dish.) Once cooked, remove the pan from the heat and let cool a little.

Preheat the oven to 400°F. Line a 6 x 12-inch ovenproof dish with nonstick parchment paper.

Crack the eggs into a large mixing bowl and whisk. Add the baking powder, flour, and yogurt, along with a little salt, if desired, and mix well. Add the barberries and pine nuts and, once the greens have cooled slightly, incorporate them into the egg mixture a little at a time, mixing well between each addition. Lastly, gently fold in the feta pieces. Pour the mixture into the prepared dish and use a spatula to ensure the ingredients are evenly distributed. Bake for 30 minutes (check after 25 minutes), or until the top is golden and beginning to brown and a knife inserted into the center comes out clean of raw egg. Let cool slightly, then cut it into slabs to serve.

WORLD'S BEST TOASTIE

When I first threw these ingredients together after a bit of a fridge forage, I didn't have much faith that the result would turn out so well. I have to say, this halloumi, honey, harissa, and tomato toastie with a pickled onion tang will satisfy cravings you didn't even know you had! Salty, sweet, juicy, and spicy—the perfect way to start (or end) a day.

9oz block of halloumi cheese, cut into
   6 equal slices

olive oil

4 slices of good-quality bread

2 teaspoons rose harissa (it's powerful
   stuff, so use moderately, unless you
   like some heat), divided

2 tablespoons honey, divided

2 tomatoes, sliced, divided

2 tablespoons "Shaken" Sweet Quick-
   Pickled Onions (*see* page 193)

3 tablespoons butter

Maldon sea salt flakes and freshly
   ground black pepper

SERVES 2

Place a skillet over medium heat, drizzle in a little olive oil, and add the halloumi slices. Fry for about 2 minutes on each side, or until golden and crusted. Meanwhile, very lightly toast your bread slices on a low setting so that they are barely browned.

Transfer the fried halloumi slices to a side plate. Use paper towels to wipe the pan clean.

Make a sandwich: place a slice of the lightly toasted bread on your work surface, then lay half the halloumi slices across it. Smear half the rose harissa over the halloumi slices. Drizzle with half of the honey. Now lay half the tomato slices across, top with some pickled onions, and season well with black pepper and a little pinch of salt (bear in mind that the halloumi is already quite salty). Top with another slice of bread, press down on the sandwich, and set aside. Make another sandwich with the remaining ingredients.

At this point, you can brush the outside of the sandwiches with the melted butter and toast them in a sandwich-maker if you have one. Alternatively, add one-quarter of the butter to the pan and let it melt over medium heat, but don't let it burn (take the pan off the heat if sizzles too much). Place one of the sandwiches in the pan. Press the toastie by placing a small saucepan on top of the sandwich with a heavy weight, such as a can, inside. Cook over medium heat for around 2 minutes, then check to see if the bread has browned. If so, raise the sandwich using a lifter, add one-third of the remaining butter, carefully turn over the sandwich, and fry the other side until browned. Take the sandwich out of the pan, repeat the process with the remaining sandwich, then serve.

SOUPS & BOWL COMFORT

CARROT, FENNEL SEED & RED LENTIL SOUP

WITH LABNEH & SESAME OIL

I admit I'm fussy when it comes to soup. A soup should be more than just warming. I like layers of flavor and different textures. It's easy to dismiss soup as a simple or easy food, when in fact the best ones are put together with some thought. Having said that, good soup needn't be complicated, expensive, or time-consuming because I believe the best things in life come together with the greatest of ease. This soup is easy to make and hits all the spots you didn't even know you had.

2 teaspoons fennel seeds

vegetable oil or ghee

1¾oz fresh ginger root, peeled and
    finely chopped or grated

1 onion, diced

1lb 2oz carrots, scrubbed and cut into
    coarse chunks

2 fat garlic cloves, coarsely chopped

1 teaspoon turmeric

2 quarts boiling water

juice of ½ lemon (about 2 tablespoons)

⅔ cup uncooked red lentils

4 tablespoons labneh or thick
    Greek yogurt, divided

4 teaspoons sesame oil, divided

Maldon sea salt flakes and freshly
    ground black pepper

couple of pinches of pul biber
    chile flakes, to garnish

SERVES 4

Toast the fennel seeds in a large, dry saucepan over medium heat for 2 minutes, then drizzle in a little vegetable oil or ghee and add the ginger and onion. Sauté until the onion begins to soften, without letting it brown. Add the carrot to the pan and stir-fry until the edges begin to soften.

Now add the garlic, turmeric, and a generous amount of salt and pepper to the saucepan and stir well. Pour in the boiling water and adjust the heat to bring the mixture to a simmer. Let simmer gently, uncovered, for 45 minutes. Let cool slightly, then blitz the mixture using a hand-held stick blender or transfer to a food processor or blender. Return the soup to the pan if necessary, adjust the seasoning, and then stir in the lemon juice.

Set the pan over medium heat and stir in the red lentils. Let simmer for 30 to 40 minutes, stirring occasionally, or until the lentils are soft. If the soup seems too thick, blitz half the mixture using the hand-held stick blender or food processor or blender.

Divide the soup among 4 bowls. Dollop 1 tablespoon labneh into each bowl and drizzle with 1 teaspoon sesame oil. Finish with a sprinkling of pul piber chili flakes and serve.

SWEET POTATO
& LIME SOUP

I love sweet potatoes in any way, shape, or form. There is something addictive about their sweet and pleasingly digestible nature I find genuinely comforting. In this delicious soup, this sweetness is balanced beautifully with fresh lime. Crumbled of feta on top makes it more of a meal.

olive oil

2 large onions, coarsely diced

4½lb sweet potatoes, peeled and
    cut into coarse chunks

2 fat garlic cloves, peeled

1 teaspoon dried wild oregano

1 teaspoon dried red chile flakes, plus
    extra to garnish

1 teaspoon turmeric

1 quart boiling water

finely grated zest of 2 unwaxed limes
    and juice of 1

Maldon sea salt flakes and freshly
    ground black pepper

7oz feta cheese, crumbled, to serve

SERVES 4 TO 6

Place a large saucepan over medium heat. Pour in enough olive oil to coat the bottom of the pan. Add the onion and cook for a few minutes until softened and translucent, without browning.

Stir the sweet potato chunks and garlic cloves into the saucepan and cook for 5 to 6 minutes, or until the edges begin to soften, without coloring.

Add the oregano and the spices, pour in the boiling water, and stir. Mix well, cover the pan with the lid, reduce the heat to medium-low, and let simmer gently for 30 minutes, or until the sweet potato is cooked through.

Transfer the mixture to a food processor or blender and blitz. If the soup seems too thick, add boiling water, a little at a time, until it reaches your desired consistency.

Return the soup to the saucepan and stir in the lime zest and juice. Season to taste, then cook for a further 15 minutes over medium-low heat.

Serve with the crumbled feta on top, a drizzle of olive oil, and extra red chile flakes, if desired.

RICE & VEGETABLE AASH
WITH PUY LENTILS

To say that aash is merely a soup would be underselling it because this hearty staple of Persian cuisine is much more than that. Always herb-based, there are many varieties: some with meat, some without; some with barley, rice, tomato, or pomegranate molasses. All are equally delicious. Aash is the best comfort food on a cold day, and virtuous enough to be the perfect meal all year round. This is my Western version, but it is still every bit as delicious.

olive oil, for frying

2 large white onions, very finely diced

1⅔ cups finely chopped flat-leaf parsley

2 cups finely chopped fresh cilantro

5 large garlic cloves, crushed

3 teaspoons unsweetened tamarind paste

2 teaspoons paprika

3 tablespoons tomato paste

⅓ cup butter

1 heaped tablespoon all-purpose flour

1 quart vegetable stock

1 quart cold water

½ cup basmati rice

½ cup uncooked Puy lentils

Maldon sea salt flakes and freshly
　　ground black pepper

To garnish

1 small pack (about 1oz) of dill,
　　finely chopped

1 bunch of scallions, thinly sliced

SERVES 6 TO 8

Place a large saucepan over medium heat. Pour in enough olive oil to coat the bottom of the pan. Add the onion and cook for a few minutes until softened and translucent, without browning.

Add the fresh herbs and cook them down for a few minutes until they are completely wilted and resemble cooked spinach. Stir in the garlic and cook for a few more minutes until soft and translucent without browning.

Add the tamarind, paprika, tomato paste, and butter to the pan, stirring them in to combine. Then add the flour and mix well. Let this fry for a few minutes, then pour in the stock and the cold water and season generously with salt and pepper.

Bring the contents of the saucepan to a rolling boil, then stir in the rice and Puy lentils. Reduce the heat and simmer uncovered for 25 to 30 minutes, or until the rice and lentils are cooked. If the soup seems too thick, add boiling water (up to 1¼ cups), a little at a time, until you reach the desired consistency. Taste and adjust the seasoning to taste, then serve immediately (it will continue to absorb more liquid if left to stand), scattered with the dill and sliced scallions.

CORN, POTATO & CHEDDAR CHOWDER

This is truly comfort in a bowl for a girl like me. Corn, potatoes, and cheese together? Seriously. What's not to love? Creamy, slightly thick, and utterly satisfying, gentle spicing gives this soup a little extra oomph. This is a full meal in a bowl, so you really won't need anything else.

olive oil

1 onion, very finely diced

1 teaspoon cumin seeds

kernels sliced from 2 cobs of corn

3 garlic cloves, bashed

1 teaspoon turmeric

2 tablespoons butter

12oz potato, peeled and coarsely grated

1 quart boiling water

5½oz sharp Cheddar cheese, grated

crème fraîche, to serve

Maldon sea salt flakes and freshly
    ground black pepper

SERVES 4 TO 6

Place a large saucepan over medium heat. Pour in enough olive oil to coat the bottom of the pan. Add the onion and cook for a few minutes until softened and translucent, without browning.

Stir in the cumin seeds and fry for 2 minutes, then add the corn, garlic, and turmeric, and cook for a few minutes until softened.

Stir the butter and grated potato into the saucepan, season with salt and pepper, and cook for 6 to 8 minutes, stirring regularly, or until the potato softens.

Pour in the boiling water, reduce the heat to low, and let simmer uncovered for 30 minutes, until the potato is cooked through. Stir in the cheese and let it melt, then ladle into bowls. Top each with a tablespoon of crème fraîche, a drizzle of olive oil, and a grinding of black pepper. Serve immediately.

ZA'ATAR, LEEK &
CELERY ROOT SOUP

I love celery root, but sometimes it needs a few extra ingredients to give it a boost. I have always found that adding za'atar to a dish only improves matters further. This is an easy soup to throw together and it delivers on flavor in a big way.

olive oil, for frying

1lb 2oz leeks, trimmed, cleaned, and coarsely chopped

1¾ to 2lb celery root, peeled and diced

3 fat garlic cloves, sliced

2 quarts boiling water

3½ tablespoons butter

2 tablespoons Za'atar Blend (see page 86)

Maldon sea salt flakes and freshly ground black pepper

SERVES 4 TO 6

Heat a large saucepan over medium heat. Drizzle in a little olive oil, add the leek, and cook for a few minutes, or until softened, without browning.

Stir in the celery root and garlic and season with pepper and a generous amount of salt. Cook for a further 12 to 15 minutes, or until the vegetables are softened. Do not let the vegetables brown (you want to keep this soup white in color). Add the boiling water, stir well, then reduce the heat to low and simmer uncovered for 30 to 40 minutes, or until the celery root is soft.

Transfer the mixture to a food processor or blender and blitz. Return the soup to the saucepan, stir in the butter until melted, then serve in bowls garnished with the za'atar and a drizzle of olive oil.

ROASTED TOMATO & CHILE SOUP

Roasting tomatoes really does intensify their flavor. If you dare, charring the edges a little improves them even more. This is one of those dishes I would recommend you double up on so that you can freeze half and gorge on it another day. Simple, full-flavored, and ever so comforting.

2¼ plum tomatoes, halved

2 long red chiles, halved lengthwise
and seeded

4 fat garlic cloves (unpeeled), wrapped
in a piece of aluminum foil to protect
them from burning

2 teaspoons cumin seeds

olive oil

2 slices of stale bread (I use sourdough),
cut into cubes

2 to 3 tablespoons Sabzi Sauce
(*see* page 195)

2 cups boiling water

1 tablespoon red wine vinegar

1 heaped teaspoon superfine sugar

Maldon sea salt flakes and freshly
ground black pepper

SERVES 2 TO 4

Preheat the oven to 375°F. Line the largest baking pan you have with nonstick parchment paper.

Arrange the tomatoes cut-side up in the prepared pan. Add to the pan the chiles and the garlic cloves in their foil. Season the tomatoes with pepper and sprinkle them with the cumin seeds. Drizzle with a generous amount of olive oil to ensure everything is coated. Roast for 45 minutes, or until the tomatoes are very soft and slightly charred. Remove from oven and let cool.

Heat a large saucepan over medium-high heat and drizzle in 2 to 3 tablespoons olive oil. Add the bread cubes and fry for a few minutes on each side, or until golden brown all over. Now drizzle the cubes with the Sabzi Sauce and toss until they are coated but retain some crunch. Remove the pan from the heat and set aside.

Transfer the roasted tomatoes, chiles, and garlic cloves (remove them from the foil and pop them out of their skins first) to a food processor or a blender and blitz until smooth. Then pour the mixture into a saucepan and add the boiling water, vinegar, sugar, and a generous amount of salt. Bring the mixture to a gentle simmer. Once hot, taste and adjust the seasoning as required, then serve immediately, with the croutons on top and an extra drizzle of olive oil, if desired.

PIES, BREADS & PASTRIES

BUTTERNUT, FETA & CHILE ROLLS

I first came up with this recipe for the launch of my second cookbook, Sirocco. I wanted something delicious and substantial for those who didn't eat meat, as well as those who did. This recipe went on to become a favorite at pop-up feasts in all sorts of different shapes and sizes. If butternut squash isn't your thing, it also works beautifully with other types of squash when in season.

2¼lb butternut squash (unpeeled), halved and seeded

olive oil

2 teaspoons dried red chile flakes

1 teaspoon ground cinnamon

1 fat garlic clove, crushed

7oz feta cheese, crumbled

1 small pack (about 1oz) of flat-leaf parsley, finely chopped

1 sheet frozen all-butter puff pastry

1 egg, beaten

1 teaspoon nigella seeds

Maldon sea salt flakes and freshly ground black pepper

MAKES 8

Preheat the oven to 415°F.

Arrange the squash halves cut-side up in a baking pan and drizzle them with a little olive oil. Roast for about 50 minutes, or until the flesh is cooked through and soft. (Don't switch off the oven.)

When cool enough to handle, use a spoon to scoop the butternut squash flesh out of the skins and into a mixing bowl. Add the chile flakes, cinnamon, and garlic, season with a generous amount of salt and pepper, then mash it all together. Now gently fold in the feta and parsley. Set aside.

Increase the oven temperature to 425°F. Line a baking pan with nonstick parchment paper.

Cut the pastry into 8 squares. Divide the filling into 8 portions. Mold one portion of filling into a sausage shape and place it diagonally across one of the pastry squares. Fold the pastry corners over the filling, pinching them together (the filling will remain exposed at each end). Repeat with the remaining pastry and filling. Transfer the parcels to the prepared pan, brush with the beaten egg, scatter with the nigella seeds, and bake for about 25 minutes or until deep golden brown. Serve hot or at room temperature according to your preference.

POTATO, SCALLION & GOAT CHEESE HAND PIES

I think that what the British don't know about savory piemaking simply isn't worth knowing, and I don't just mean meat pies. Some of the best, most comforting pies are meat-free, such as the classic homity pie. Filled with nothing more than potato, cheese, leek, and onion, it is quite possibly one of my favorite pies of all time. This recipe combines similar ingredients in a simple puff-pastry crust, perfect for summer bites and winter nights.

½lb new potatoes

9oz soft goat cheese

1 tablespoon dried wild oregano

3 fat scallions, thinly sliced from root to tip

½ small pack (about ½oz) of tarragon, leaves finely chopped

1 sheet frozen all-butter puff pastry

1 egg, beaten

1 teaspoon nigella seeds

Maldon sea salt flakes and freshly ground black pepper

MAKES 6

Boil the potatoes for 15 minutes, then drain and let cool.

Halve the cooled potatoes lengthwise down the center, then slice each potato half into half-moons.

Put the goat cheese, oregano, scallions, and a good amount of salt and pepper into a large mixing bowl and mash the ingredients together. Then add the potato pieces and tarragon. Stir well to combine.

Preheat the oven to 400°F. Line a large baking pan with nonstick parchment paper.

Unroll the pastry and cut it into 6 squares. Divide the filling into 6 portions and shape each portion into a ball. Place a ball of filling in the center of each pastry square, then gather up the pastry corners and pinch them together to seal (it doesn't need to be perfect). Transfer the parcels to the prepared baking pan, brush with the beaten egg, scatter with the nigella seeds, and bake for 25 to 30 minutes, or until golden brown. Serve immediately.

ROAST VEGETABLE BASTILLA

Bastilla is traditionally a celebratory Moroccan dish made with pigeon, but I've made this with leftover roasted vegetables, which is how this version was born. You can pretty much throw anything together with Moroccan spices, dried fruit, and nuts and turn it into something beautiful. This makes an impressive centerpiece, yet it is ridiculously easy to make.

1 teaspoon cayenne pepper

2 teaspoons ground cinnamon

2 teaspoons turmeric

2 teaspoons ground cumin

2 teaspoons garlic granules

1lb 10oz celery root, peeled and cut into
   1-inch cubes

1lb 10oz butternut squash, peeled,
   seeded, and cut into 1-inch cubes

1lb 2oz carrots, peeled and cut into
   1-inch chunks

1lb 2oz parsnips, peeled and cut into
   1-inch chunks

olive oil

½ cup sliced almonds

⅓ cup pine nuts

½ cup ready-to-eat dried apricots,
   coarsely chopped

1 cup finely chopped flat-leaf parsley

¼ cup honey

finely grated zest and juice of
   1 unwaxed lemon

6 sheets of filo pastry (each about
   19 x 10 inches)

⅓ cup butter, melted

1 egg, beaten

Maldon sea salt flakes and freshly
   ground black pepper

SERVES 6 TO 8

Preheat the oven to 425°F. Line your 2 largest baking pans with nonstick parchment paper.

Mix all the spices and garlic granules together in a bowl. Put the vegetables into a large mixing bowl. Sprinkle them with the spice blend, drizzle liberally with olive oil, and season generously with salt and pepper. Then use your hands to mix until the vegetables are well coated. Divide the mixture between the 2 prepared pans and roast for about 45 minutes, opening the oven door briefly halfway through the cooking time to let the steam escape. Once the edges of the vegetables start to brown, remove from the oven and let cool. At this point you can refrigerate the vegetables to use later.

Coarsely chop the cooled root vegetables and put them into a large mixing bowl along with the nuts, dried apricots, parsley, honey, and lemon zest and juice. Add a generous extra seasoning of salt and mix well using a large spoon, ensuring you don't mash the vegetables too much (but mashing them a little is actually quite nice!).

Preheat the oven to 425°F. Line the largest baking pan you have with nonstick parchment paper.

Select a large skillet, about 10 inches in diameter. Line it with a pastry sheet, leaving the end hanging over (you need plenty of overhang to be able to fold this over the top of the filling), then lay the remaining pastry sheets on top in a clockwise direction. Tip the filling mixture into the center and flatten it out to make a firm disk. Fold the overhanging pastry over the filling and brush with the melted butter to seal the pastry together.

Place the prepared baking pan upside-down over the skillet and, holding the baking pan and skillet firmly together, quickly invert the bastilla onto the baking pan. Lift the skillet off and brush the top of the pastry with the beaten egg. Bake for 25 to 30 minutes, or until golden brown. Serve immediately.

CARAMELIZED ONION, FETA & OLIVE TART

Savory tarts are so versatile. You can bake one for dinner, then serve the leftovers with a salad for lunch the next day. It's lovely for breakfast or brunch, too, and it makes a fantastic addition as part of a bigger feast. Tarts are easy to make. I sometimes cheat and use store-bought pie pastry if I'm short of time (use a 1lb block of ready-made pie pastry, then roll it out and bake as in the method below). If you're making the pastry, prepare a double batch of dough and freeze half; it'll make life so much easier next time you make a tart.

1¾ cups all-purpose flour, plus
    extra for dusting
½ cup cold salted butter, cut into
    small cubes
3 to 4 tablespoons cold water

For the filling
vegetable oil
2 large onions, halved and thinly sliced
    into half-moons
1 teaspoon wild thyme leaves
9oz ricotta cheese
7oz feta cheese, finely crumbled
1 large egg
1 teaspoon pul biber chile flakes
1 teaspoon garlic granules
16 pitted Kalamata olives, plus a few
    extra to garnish
pinch of Maldon sea salt flakes
freshly ground black pepper

SERVES 8 TO 10

First make the pastry. Put the flour into a large mixing bowl, then rub in the butter with your fingertips until the mixture resembles fine bread crumbs. Add the cold water and mix to a stiff dough. Roll the dough into a ball, seal it in plastic wrap, and refrigerate for at least 30 minutes.

To make the filling, drizzle a little vegetable oil into a large skillet set over medium-low heat. Add the onion and thyme and cook slowly, stirring regularly, until the onion has caramelized and is golden in color. Do not allow it to crisp up or burn. Once cooked, set aside to cool.

Select a 9½-inch pie plate. Place a large square of plastic wrap on your work surface. Dust generously with flour, then set the dough on top, dust that with flour, and cover it loosely with more plastic wrap. Roll out the dough until it is slightly larger than your pie plate (the dough should be nice and thin). Remove the top layer of plastic wrap and carefully transfer the dough into the pie plate. Don't worry if it breaks; you can easily patch it up later with dough trimmings. Push the dough gently into the edges of the pie plate, leaving a little overhanging. Now sweep the rolling pin across the top of the pie plate to cut off the overhanging dough. Use the trimmings to patch up any cracks or holes. Cover with plastic wrap and refrigerate for at least 20 minutes.

Preheat the oven to 400°F.

In a mixing bowl, combine the ricotta, feta, and egg until the mixture is smooth. Add the pul biber, garlic granules, olives, and caramelized onions, and season with the salt and a generous amount of black pepper. Stir well to combine.

Pour the filling into the pastry-lined pie plate and garnish with a few extra olives, if desired. Bake for 30 to 35 minutes, or until cooked through and brown on top. Let cool slightly before serving.

DATE-STUFFED NAAN

Many years ago I worked at a Michelin-starred Indian restaurant, and the one thing I've never forgotten is their mind-blowing date naan. Sadly, I never learned how to make it, but the memory of its chocolate-like filling against chewy, charred bread has stayed with me and inspired this date bread. Although my version is not fired in a Tandoor clay oven, it is still every bit as satisfying.

2¾ cups strong bread flour, plus extra
    for dusting

¼oz envelope instant yeast

good pinch of Maldon sea salt flakes

⅔ cup Greek yogurt

½ cup lukewarm water, plus extra
    if needed

2 tablespoons olive oil

1 tablespoon sesame seeds

1½ tablespoons unsalted butter, melted

For the filling

10½oz best-quality dates, stoned and
    coarsely chopped

3½ tablespoons unsalted butter

2 tablespoons honey

1 tablespoon ground cinnamon

SERVES 6 TO 8

Mix the flour, yeast, and salt together in a large mixing bowl, then add the yogurt, measured lukewarm water, and olive oil. Use your hands to combine the mixture in a dough, adding a little extra flour or water, if needed, to bring the dough together. Knead the dough in the bowl for 1 minute, then let rest for 10 minutes. Knead the dough again for 1 minute, then cover the bowl with a clean dishcloth and let stand somewhere warm for 1½ hours to rise.

Put the filling ingredients into a small saucepan over medium-low heat and cook for a few minutes until heated through. Take the pan off the heat and mash the mixture to a paste. This should happen fairly easily, as the dates will break down quickly. Set aside.

Preheat the oven to 425°F. Line your largest baking pan with nonstick parchment paper.

Once the dough has risen, punch it down and divide it into 2 equal balls. Lightly dust your work surface with flour and roll out each ball of dough to a thickness of just under ¼ inch, in any shape you like—circular or irregular—but ensure they are both roughly the same shape.

Lay one sheet of dough on the prepared pan. Spread the date paste across it, leaving a border of 1 inch. Place the other sheet of dough on top and tuck the edges under the first sheet of dough, then pinch the edges together to seal the parcel as best you can. Lastly, scatter it with the sesame seeds, pressing them into the dough (a rolling pin helps with this). Now brush the dough all over with the melted butter, ensuring you brush right to the edges. Bake for 18 to 20 minutes, or until the naan is cooked through and nicely browned on top. Let cool before serving.

PERSIAN SWEET SAFFRON BREAD

Sheermal is a sweet, saffron-tinted Persian bread and a treasured memory from my childhood in London when the local Persian restaurants sold them. Now they're impossible to find. This is my own lighter version—no kneading is required—and I would encourage you to eat it with spicy dishes such as curries, soups, and stews, although a bit of feta and a drizzle of honey would also do nicely.

a pinch of saffron threads, ground to a powder using a mortar and pestle

3 tablespoons boiling water

2½ cups strong bread flour, plus extra for dusting

⅛oz (½ envelope) instant yeast

good pinch of Maldon sea salt flakes

¼ cup superfine sugar

¼ cup butter, melted

⅔ cup milk, plus extra for glazing

1 teaspoon black or white sesame seeds

MAKES 4

Put the saffron powder into a small cup and add the boiling water. Let steep until the liquid is cool.

Put the flour, yeast, salt, and sugar into a large mixing bowl and stir to combine. Add the melted butter, milk, and the cooled saffron solution and stir well to form a dough. Roll the dough into a smooth ball and place it in a bowl. Cover the bowl with plastic wrap, then cover with a clean dishcloth and let stand somewhere warm for 1½ hours to rise.

Preheat the oven to 400°F. Line a large baking sheet with nonstick parchment paper.

Once the dough has risen, punch it down and divide it into 4 equal portions. Lightly dust your work surface with flour and roll out each portion of dough into a disk roughly ½ inch in thickness. Transfer the disks to the prepared baking sheet. Brush the surfaces with milk, then sprinkle each one with one-quarter of the sesame seeds. Bake for 12 to 15 minutes, or until brown around the edges. Transfer to a wire rack to cool, then serve warm.

ZA'ATAR-RUBBED PITTAS

This is my take on a popular Lebanese flatbread snack called maneesh. If I'm honest, I have a pitta addiction, and rubbing the top of pitta bread with za'atar and olive oil is absolutely delicious. Za'atar wasn't something I used much until I became a chef, and I never fully understood its potential until I started using it at home. This versatile herb blend can be used with bread, salads, and cheese, as well as in marinades and rubs, and so much more.

For the za'atar blend

¼ cup dried wild thyme

⅓ cup dried wild oregano

⅓ cup dried marjoram

2 tablespoons sumac

2 tablespoons sesame seeds,
  lightly toasted

1 tablespoon Maldon sea salt flakes

MAKES 1 JAR

3 tablespoons olive oil, for the za'atar oil

For the pitta bread

⅛oz (½ envelope) instant yeast

⅔ cup lukewarm water

2 cups all-purpose flour, plus extra
  for dusting

1 teaspoon fine sea salt

2 tablespoons olive oil

MAKES 6

To make the za'atar blend, use a spice or coffee grinder to grind the thyme, oregano, and marjoram together just until they break down (you can also use a mortar and pestle, but it won't work as well). Decant the mixture into a bowl, stir in the sumac, sesame seeds, and salt, then pour into an airtight container. It will last for up to a year if stored in a dark, cool, dry place.

To make a za'atar oil, combine 4 teaspoons of the za'atar blend with the olive oil. Stir well and set aside.

To make the pitta bread, dissolve the yeast in the lukewarm water and let stand for 5 minutes. Put the flour, salt, and olive oil into a mixing bowl, add the yeast mixture and mix together with your hands to form a dough. Knead the dough in the bowl for a few minutes, then cover the bowl with plastic wrap and let stand somewhere warm for 1 hour to rise.

Divide the dough into 6 equal balls. Lightly dust your work surface with flour and roll out each ball of dough into a disk about ¼ inch thick. Let the disks rest for 10 minutes.

When you are ready to cook the pitta bread, place a large heavy skillet over medium-high heat. When the skillet is hot, place a dough disk into it (without any oil) and cook for about 45 seconds on one side, or until the edges begin to come away from the pan. Then flip it over and cook for a further 30 to 45 seconds, or until very lightly browned. Keep the pitta warm while you cook the remaining dough disks in the same way.

Divide the za'atar oil equally between the 6 hot pittas and rub it into the surface. Serve immediately.

SALADS FOR
ALL SEASONS

BLACKBERRY, BEET & ZA'ATAR GOAT CHEESE SALAD

Nothing reminds me more of England than all the gorgeous berries and autumnal fruit we produce in abundance. I like to combine Middle Eastern ingredients with Western produce if the flavors work, and this combination does exactly that with sweet but tart blackberries with creamy soft goat-cheese balls dusted in my beloved herb mix, za'atar. This is now one of my favorite fall salads, and once you try it, you'll see why.

7oz soft goat cheese

2 to 3 tablespoons Za'atar Blend
   (*see* page 86)

5½oz mixed salad leaves

10½oz cooked beets (not in vinegar),
   quartered

9oz blackberries (reserve 6 for the
   dressing)

freshly ground black pepper

For the dressing

6 blackberries (reserved from the salad
   ingredients)

1 tablespoon red wine vinegar

2 tablespoons olive oil

pinch of Maldon sea salt flakes

SERVES 4 TO 6

First make the dressing. In a small bowl or using a mortar and pestle, bash 6 of the blackberries until puréed, then add the vinegar, olive oil, and salt. Mix well and set aside.

To prepare the salad, divide the goat cheese into 12 equal-sized cubes and roll them into smooth balls. Lightly dust with the za'atar blend then roll each between your palms to ensure the za'atar sticks to the surface. Set the balls on a plate and refrigerate until needed.

When you're ready to serve, select a large, wide board or platter and spread the salad greens across it. Arrange the beet quarters and the blackberries around the board or plate, then season with pepper and drizzle with the dressing. Lastly, dot with the goat cheese balls and serve immediately.

MILLI'S CHARRED CORN SALAD

Once in a blue moon, I sheepishly agree to cook a meal for a talented chef friend of mine named Milli Taylor. Milli is one of those doubly talented individuals who not only makes food that tastes amazing, but her creations look beautiful, too. She always enjoys my salads, and this one in particular—a rainbow salad, as she calls it. She has good taste (it's also a favorite of mine).

2 cobs of corn

14oz can hearts of palm, drained and cut diagonally into slices ½ inch thick

10½oz baby tomatoes, halved

½ red onion, sliced into half-moons

½ small pack (about ½oz) of fresh cilantro, coarsely chopped

For the dressing

3 tablespoons Greek yogurt

1 tablespoon harissa

juice of ½ fat lime

Maldon sea salt flakes and freshly ground black pepper

SERVES 4 TO 6

Mix the dressing ingredients together in a small bowl and season to taste with salt and pepper. Set aside.

Cook the corn on the cob in a saucepan of simmering water for 10 minutes, or until soft but not completely tender, then drain. Preheat a ridged grill pan over high heat and char the corn cobs for 5 minutes, turning occasionally, until blackened in places. Remove from the heat and transfer to a cutting board. Hold the cobs vertically and, using a sharp knife, cut down to slice off the kernels. Then add them to a mixing bowl.

Arrange the hearts of palm, corn kernels, tomato halves, and red onion slices on a serving platter. Dot with the dressing, scatter with cilantro, and serve.

CRUNCHY TOFU SALAD
WITH TAMARIND & MISO DRESSING

I am a recent convert to tofu and have concluded that it is an excellent carrier of flavor. When combined with some carefully selected punchy ingredients—in this instance a lovely crisp and crunchy salad base—it is absolutely perfect.

3 cups finely shredded white cabbage

3 cups red cabbage, finely shredded

1 small red pepper, cored, seeded, and cut into thin strips

1 small yellow pepper, cored, seeded, and cut into thin strips

3 celery stalks, very thinly sliced

4 scallions, thinly sliced diagonally from root to tip

⅔ cup salted roasted peanuts

1 small pack (about 1oz) of fresh cilantro, coarsely chopped

14oz firm tofu, cut into 1-inch cubes

For the dressing

3 tablespoons unsweetened tamarind paste

3 tablespoons white miso paste

3 tablespoons honey

3 tablespoons olive oil

1 teaspoon cayenne pepper

1 teaspoon ground cinnamon

finely grated zest and juice of ½ unwaxed lemon

Maldon sea salt flakes and freshly ground black pepper

SERVES 4

Preheat a nonstick ridged grill pan over high heat.

Meanwhile, combine all the salad ingredients, except the tofu, in a large mixing bowl.

Mix the dressing ingredients together in a small bowl and season well with salt and pepper.

Place the tofu cubes in a shallow bowl and dress them with approximately one-third of the dressing. Pour the remainder of the dressing over the salad and toss the salad with your hands to ensure the ingredients are well coated.

Chargrill the tofu pieces for about 1 minute on each side, or until dark char marks appear.

Transfer the salad to a large wide bowl, dot with the grilled tofu, and serve.

ORANGE, OLIVE & ONION SALAD

I am one of those weirdos who is obsessed with transforming vegetables into sweet dishes and adding fruit to savory salads. The truth is, nothing beats a refreshing, juicy burst of fruit to complement the kind of food that I make. More importantly, the gentle sweetness and acidity cut through spice and chile heat perfectly. This particular salad is a great favorite of mine, as I am forever zesting oranges for all sorts of recipes and often left with the whole fruit. This is the perfect way to use them up.

4 oranges (blood oranges are a great
    choice, when in season)
½ red onion, very thinly sliced into
    half-moons
2 handfuls of green olives, pitted
few sprigs of mint, leaves picked,
    rolled up tightly, and thinly sliced
    into ribbons
good handful of pine nuts
2 pinches of pul biber chile flakes
extra virgin olive oil, for drizzling
Maldon sea salt flakes and freshly
    ground black pepper

SERVES 4 TO 6

You'll need a sharp knife to peel the oranges. With each fruit, cut a round disk of peel off the top and base of the orange. Then, working from the top of the fruit downward, cut away the remaining peel and pith in strips until the entire orange is peeled. Slice the orange widthwise into 4 or 5 round slices.

Arrange the orange slices on a large platter or board. Season well with salt and pepper, then scatter with the onion slivers, followed by the olives, fresh mint, and pine nuts. Sprinkle with the pul biber. Drizzle with a little olive oil and serve immediately.

ROOT RIBBON SALAD

WITH POMEGRANATE

I've always said that if I have to eat a salad, it had better have a lot going for it flavorwise. I've also realized that the crunchier you make a salad, the more you chew, and the quicker you feel full. I do wish the same rule applied to eating pies and heavier food, but that's life, right? This wonderfully sweet-tasting salad is packed full of flavor, crunch, and visual appeal. Hard to beat, really.

½ small white cabbage, finely shredded

1¼ cups dried cranberries

1 bunch of scallions, finely sliced
  diagonally from root to tip

1 cup toasted cashew nuts

2 large parsnips, peeled and cut into
  ribbons with a vegetable peeler

2 large carrots, peeled and cut into
  ribbons with a vegetable peeler

½ small celery root, peeled and cut into
  ribbons with a vegetable peeler

½ cup fresh dill, finely chopped

½ cup mint, leaves picked, rolled up
  tightly, and thinly sliced into ribbons

1 cup pomegranate seeds

For the dressing

1 heaped teaspoon cumin seeds, toasted
  and coarsely crushed using
  a mortar and pestle

1 heaped teaspoon coriander seeds,
  toasted and coarsely crushed using
  a mortar and pestle

1 heaped tablespoon rose harissa

3 tablespoons rice wine vinegar

2 to 3 tablespoons honey

good drizzle of extra virgin olive oil

Maldon sea salt flakes and freshly
  ground black pepper

SERVES 6 TO 8

Mix the dressing ingredients together in a small bowl and season to taste with salt and pepper.

Put the cabbage, cranberries, scallion, cashew nuts, and the dressing into a large mixing bowl and mix well with your hands. Add the parsnip, carrot, and celery root ribbons and mix again. Now add the herbs and pomegranate seeds and toss through. Check the seasoning and adjust if necessary, then toss one last time and serve immediately.

SPICED BUTTERMILK SALAD

The first time I saw a Caesar salad served with quartered heads of lettuce, I was horrified! Since then, I have come to embrace the "lazy lettuce method," as I now call it. While this isn't a classic Caesar (it pains me to eat a salad with more calories and fat than a burger), it is a lovely variation, and the eggs make it a complete and rather filling meal.

4 eggs

2 pitta breads

2 large Romaine lettuce, quartered lengthwise

1 long shallot, thinly sliced

4 radishes, thinly sliced

1 heaped teaspoon sumac

For the spiced buttermilk dressing

1¼ cups buttermilk

1 teaspoon ground coriander

1 teaspoon garlic granules

½ teaspoon celery salt

1 generous tablespoon olive oil

freshly ground black pepper

SERVES 4

First make the buttermilk dressing. Mix the buttermilk, coriander, garlic granules, celery salt, and olive oil in a small bowl and season with some black pepper. Set aside.

Half-fill a saucepan with water, cover, and set over medium-high heat. Once the water reaches a rolling boil, carefully lower in the eggs and boil for 6 minutes. Drain the eggs, then place them under cold running water to arrest the cooking process. When they are cool enough to handle, peel and then halve each egg.

Toast the pitta breads in a toaster until they have dried out, then cut into small cubes. (Alternatively, cut the pitta into cubes, place on a baking pan, and bake in a preheated oven at 350°F for 12 minutes.)

Arrange the lettuce quarters in a large serving dish. Arrange the egg halves in the bowl, followed by the sliced shallots and radishes. Drizzle with the dressing, sprinkle with the sumac for a final flourish, and serve.

BLOOD ORANGE, PECAN & CANNELLINI SALAD

WITH SAUTÉED FENNEL

Vibrant, refreshing, satisfying, and delicious: all the things I want from a salad. This one is perfect served as a main meal or a side dish. Being a colorful creation, it makes a great centerpiece at any time of year, whether you use blood oranges or not.

olive oil

2 large fennel bulbs, quartered, then cut into slices roughly ¼ inch in thickness

4 best-quality blood oranges (or use normal oranges)

3½oz mixed salad leaves (Continental or Italian mix; arugula and watercress work especially well)

14oz can cannellini beans, drained and rinsed

1 cup pecans

⅔ cup golden raisins

1 small pack (about ¼oz) of chives, each stem snipped into thirds

Maldon sea salt flakes and freshly ground black pepper

For the dressing

2 tablespoons red wine vinegar

1 tablespoon honey

1 teaspoon ground cinnamon

½ teaspoon cayenne pepper (optional)

1 tablespoon water

generous drizzle of extra virgin olive oil

Maldon sea salt flakes and freshly ground black pepper

SERVES 4 TO 6

Set a large skillet over medium heat and drizzle in a little olive oil. Add the fennel slices and sauté for a few minutes, until slightly softened and the edges turn golden brown. Transfer to a bowl using a slotted spoon, season with a little salt and pepper, and set aside.

You'll need a sharp knife to peel the oranges. With each fruit, cut a round disk of peel off the top and base of the orange. Then, working from the top of the fruit downward, cut off the remaining peel and pith in strips until the entire orange is peeled. Slice the orange widthwise into slices ½ inch thick.

Arrange the mixed leaves on a large platter or in a shallow salad bowl. Scatter the leaves with the cannellini beans and arrange the orange slices and pecans across the salad. Add the fennel, then scatter the salad with the raisins and chives.

Mix the dressing ingredients together in a small bowl, then drizzle the dressing over the salad. Serve immediately.

ROASTED PEPPERS & POMEGRANATE VINAIGRETTE

I love roasting peppers. Since I have never had a gas stove in my kitchen, or an outdoor space to barbecue at home (yes, I know; shock horror!), I roast them in the oven. It's easy, and I think they are just as good as chargrilled ones. A subtle element of vinegar complements their intense sweetness, and, with the added crunch and earthy flavor of pistachio, this dish is one of the most simple yet intensely flavored salads there is.

1lb 2oz small or baby mixed peppers or 6 long pointed red or yellow peppers, halved, cored, and seeded

3 tablespoons olive oil

½ cup coarsely chopped pistachios

Maldon sea salt flakes

For the dressing

3 tablespoons pomegranate molasses

2 tablespoons red wine vinegar

2 tablespoons olive oil

Maldon sea salt flakes

SERVES 6

Preheat your oven to its highest temperature setting. Line a baking pan with nonstick parchment paper.

Arrange the peppers skin-side up on the prepared baking pan. Drizzle them with the olive oil, season well with salt, and roast in the oven for 14 to 16 minutes, or until nicely charred.

Mix the ingredients for the dressing together in a small bowl and season with a little salt to taste.

Arrange the peppers on a platter and spoon the dressing evenly over them. Scatter with the pistachios and serve.

CABBAGE & SESAME SALAD

White cabbage is hugely underrated. Although it is most commonly used in coleslaw, it has so much more potential. It is the Japanese use of simple shredded cabbage on the side of katsu (all things bread-crumbed and fried) that inspired this salad, which has a great depth of flavor and is very moreish.

1¼ to 1½lb white cabbage,
    finely shredded
1 tablespoon nigella seeds
⅓ cup toasted sesame seeds
2 teaspoons pul biber chile flakes

For the dressing
1 tablespoon sesame oil
3 tablespoons rice vinegar
2 heaped tablespoons tahini
1 tablespoon honey
Maldon sea salt flakes and freshly
    ground black pepper

SERVES 6 TO 8

Put the shredded cabbage into a large mixing bowl.

To make the dressing, mix the sesame oil, vinegar, and tahini together in a small bowl, using a light touch because tahini stiffens if you overmix it. Stir in the honey and season with a generous amount of salt and pepper.

Pour the dressing evenly over the cabbage and mix well. Add the nigella and sesame seeds and pul biber, mix again, then serve immediately.

ZUCCHINI, PEA & SPINACH SALAD
WITH PRESERVED LEMON DRESSING

This is one of those salads that is so green and vibrant you just know you are being healthy eating it, but moreover, it has a wonderful flavor and texture. The sharp spike of preserved lemons gives it the perfect tang and the crunchy pumpkin seeds finish it off. It's just the perfect summer salad. I sometimes eat this stirred through cold cooked pasta with a little extra feta and some olive oil for a more filling meal.

1 cup fresh peas

½ cup pumpkin seeds

2 zucchini, coarsely grated

5½oz baby spinach

For the dressing

2 teaspoons coriander seeds

4 preserved lemons

¼ cup olive oil

freshly ground black pepper

SERVES 4 TO 6

Bring a small saucepan of water to a boil, add the peas, and blanch for 2 minutes. Drain the peas and rinse them in cold water, then drain well and set aside.

Toast the coriander seeds for the dressing in a dry skillet over medium heat for about 1 minute, until they release their aroma. Remove from the heat, transfer to a mortar and pestle, and crush them lightly, grinding just enough to crack the seeds.

In the same skillet, toast the pumpkin seeds for 3 to 4 minutes, or until they are slightly charred around the edges and have some color. Transfer to a bowl and set aside to cool.

To make the dressing, you can either chop the preserved lemons very finely and purée them by hand using a mortar and pestle, or blitz them in a mini blender. Transfer them to a bowl, season with black pepper, stir in the olive oil, then the crushed coriander seeds, and mix well (you won't need salt, as the preserved lemons are already salty).

Put the grated zucchini, spinach, and the peas into a large mixing bowl, pour in the dressing, and toss very lightly using your hands until the leaves are coated. Arrange the dressed leaves on a large platter and scatter with the roasted pumpkin seeds. Serve immediately.

RED & WHITE RICE SALAD
WITH BUTTERNUT SQUASH & POMEGRANATE

This is what my family knows as my Thanksgiving salad. Despite being British, many of my family are based in the US and we need no excuse to gather en masse at any time of the year. This salad is my annual contribution to the festivities. I always make a ridiculously huge amount so it can be given away to various people to take with them.

2¼ to 2½lb butternut squash, peeled, seeded, and cut into 1-inch cubes

olive oil

3 tablespoons cumin seeds

¾ cup basmati rice

¾ cup red Camargue rice

1¾ cups dried cranberries

1 cup toasted sliced almonds

2 cups finely chopped flat-leaf parsley

1 large red onion, very finely diced

finely grated zest and juice of 1 large unwaxed orange

2 teaspoons ground cinnamon

¼ to ⅓ cup red wine vinegar

¼ cup honey

1½ cups pomegranate seeds

Maldon sea salt flakes and freshly ground black pepper

SERVES 6 TO 8

Preheat the oven to 425°F. Line a baking pan with nonstick parchment paper.

Place the butternut squash pieces on the prepared baking pan and drizzle generously with olive oil. Scatter with the cumin seeds and season generously with salt and pepper. Mix using your hands to ensure each cube is evenly coated in the oil and seasoning. Roast for 40 to 45 minutes, or until the edges of the squash are browned and charred. Once cooked, set aside to cool.

Bring 2 saucepans of water to a boil and cook the 2 different varieties of rice following the package directions. Drain and rinse thoroughly under cold running water until completely cool, then drain well.

Put the cranberries, almonds, parsley, onion, and rice into a large mixing bowl and stir to combine. Add the orange zest and juice, cinnamon, ⅓ cup of olive oil, the vinegar, and honey. Season generously with salt and pepper and stir well. Gently incorporate the cubes of cooled butternut squash into the salad along with the pomegranate seeds. Arrange the salad in a very large bowl and serve at room temperature.

MOGHRABIEH SALAD

Despite its exotic name, moghrabieh is essentially giant couscous, or small dots of pasta. Infinitely versatile, it works very well in stews, soups, salads, and on its own as a main dish, as you might serve a pilaf. This lovely salad is great at any time of year. Perfect for warmer weather, with gentle spicing and comfort it's great for the colder months, too. The golden raisins give a wonderful burst of sweetness to every bite. This salad is even better the next day, so make it the day before and refrigerate to allow the spices to intensify.

2 cups moghrabieh (giant couscous)

2 tablespoons olive oil

1 large red pepper, cored, seeded, and cut into ½-inch dice

1 large yellow pepper, cored, seeded, and cut into ½-inch dice

⅔ cup pine nuts

2 small packs (about 2¼oz) of dill, finely chopped

2 cups coarsely chopped flat-leaf parsley

Maldon sea salt flakes and freshly ground black pepper

For the dressing

3 tablespoons olive oil

3 tablespoons red wine vinegar

3 tablespoons honey

2 teaspoons ground cinnamon

1 teaspoon dried red chile flakes

SERVES 6 TO 8

Boil the moghrabieh following the package directions. Drain the grains and rinse them thoroughly under cold running water until completely cool, then drain well. Set aside.

Heat the olive oil in a saucepan over medium-high heat. Add the peppers and sauté for about 8 minutes, or until soft and browned at the edges. Set aside to cool.

Place a small skillet over medium heat and add the pine nuts. Toast for a few minutes, shaking the pan, until golden all over, then remove from the heat and set aside.

Mix the dressing ingredients together in a small bowl and set aside.

Put the cooked moghrabieh into a large bowl. Add the peppers, herbs, and pine nuts and mix well until they are evenly distributed. Season generously with salt and pepper. Now pour in the dressing and stir. Let stand for at least 30 minutes to allow the flavors to develop before serving.

SMOKED EGGPLANT, PEPPER & WALNUT SALAD
WITH POMEGRANATE

I always associate smoked eggplant with the East. Most Middle Eastern nations seem to have a version of them, and the roots of many of these recipes relate to the world's most simple and primitive cooking technique—food plus fire—which as we all know equals nothing short of magic. From meat to every kind of vegetable and even some fruits, very few edibles aren't somehow improved by the kiss of fire, and eggplant is definitely my favorite.

4 large eggplants

3 large red peppers

½ cup chopped walnuts

1 small pack (about 1oz) of flat-leaf parsley, coarsely chopped (reserve some for garnish)

2 fat garlic cloves, crushed

⅓ cup olive oil, plus extra to serve

juice of ½ lemon

pinch of ground cinnamon

⅓ cup pomegranate molasses

½ cup pomegranate seeds

Maldon sea salt flakes and freshly ground black pepper

flatbread, to serve (*see* page 38)

SERVES 6 TO 8

Blister and char the eggplants and peppers, either on a barbecue, flame grill, or on the flame of your gas stove. Really blacken the skins until they are hardened and completely burnt. (Lining your stove with foil will prevent you having to deal with a very heavy cleanup, as the juices can be messy.)

Place the eggplants on a heatproof surface or baking pan and let cool for about 20 minutes until they are just warm and you are able to handle them.

Place the peppers in a food bag, tie it shut, and set aside to let them sweat for about 20 minutes. Once this time has elapsed, the blackened, charred skins should slide easily off until you are left with just the roasted flesh. Coarsely chop the flesh and place in a large mixing bowl.

Using a large metal spoon, scoop the flesh out of the eggplants and place it in a wire sieve to drain off any of the excess juices. Discard the charred skins. Coarsely chop the flesh into smallish chunks and add them to the roasted peppers. Mix together gently.

Add the walnuts, parsley, garlic, olive oil, lemon juice, cinnamon, and salt and pepper to the bowl. Give all the ingredients a good stir until they are evenly combined.

Serve the eggplant smoothed out flat on a large platter. Drizzle with the pomegranate molasses, scatter with the reserved parsley and the pomegranate seeds, then drizzle lightly with olive oil. Serve immediately with flatbread.

MOREISH MAINS

SMOKY BLACK-EYED PEA & TOMATO STEW

Simplicity is best. That's what I had in mind when I came up with the recipe for this stew, the sum of which is far greater than the parts. It provides the most perfect, comforting bowl of warmth. It's welcome as a lunch or dinner, and any leftovers on toast topped off with an egg make a great breakfast. A little cheese on top works wonders, but I really like it just as it comes, perhaps with a hunk of crusty bread on the side.

olive oil

2 onions, finely chopped

4 fat garlic cloves, thinly sliced

1 teaspoon dried red chile flakes

1 teaspoon ground cinnamon

1 teaspoon smoked paprika

2 teaspoons ground cumin

2 teaspoons unsweetened cocoa powder

2 x 14oz cans diced tomatoes
    (reserve the liquid from 1 can,
    drain the second can)

2 x 14oz cans black-eyed peas,
    drained and rinsed

Maldon sea salt flakes and freshly
    ground black pepper

SERVES 4 TO 6

Add enough olive oil to coat the bottom of a large saucepan and set over medium heat. Add the onion and cook for 6 to 8 minutes, or until softened and translucent. Stir in the garlic and cook for a few more minutes until softened.

Add all the spices, the cocoa powder, and a generous amount of salt and pepper to the saucepan and stir well. Mix in the tomatoes, then reduce the heat, cover the pan, and let simmer gently for another 30 minutes, or until the tomato has thickened and cooked down to a sauce.

Taste the stew and adjust the seasoning if necessary, then stir in the black-eyed peas. If the stew is too thick, use a little of the reserved canning liquid from the tomatoes to loosen the sauce. Cook for 15 to 20 minutes to warm the black-eyed peas through and allow them to take on the flavors of the spices, then serve.

CHICKPEA, PANEER, SPINACH, & PRESERVED LEMON STEW

This full-flavored stew is delicious and the preserved lemons give it a lovely citrus zing. A little bread or rice on the side is all you need to provide the perfect vehicle for the soft morsels of paneer.

vegetable oil

2 onions, halved and sliced into
   half-moons

1 heaped teaspoon turmeric

2 tablespoons dried mint

1 large garlic bulb, cloves peeled

1lb 2oz baby spinach

14oz can chickpeas

1 cup boiling water

6 to 8 preserved lemons, halved

8oz paneer, cut into 12 cubes

Maldon sea salt flakes and freshly
   ground black pepper

SERVES 4 TO 6

Put a drizzle of vegetable oil into a large saucepan set over medium heat. Add the onion and cook for 6 to 8 minutes, or until softened. Stir in the turmeric and mint and cook for 1 minute, then mix in the garlic cloves. Cook for a few minutes until the garlic has softened a little, then stir in the spinach. Cover the pan with a lid and cook for 2 to 3 minutes, or until the spinach has wilted.

Season the mixture in the saucepan generously with salt and pepper, then add the chickpeas and stir in the boiling water. Reduce the heat to low, partially cover the pan with the lid, and let simmer for 20 minutes until it has thickened to a broth and is not too watery.

Check the seasoning and adjust it if necessary, then mix the preserved lemon halves into the saucepan. Now stir in the paneer. Cook for a further 15 minutes, then serve immediately with bread or rice.

HARISSA PASTA DOUGH

In case you need more proof of the versatility of harissa, this fresh pasta has so much flavor that I'd happily serve it with just a little butter and some cheese because it's so delicious.

1¾ cups "00" flour, plus extra as
    required and for dusting
2 eggs
¼ cup rose harissa
good pinch of Maldon sea salt flakes

SERVES 2 TO 4

Put all the ingredients into a large bowl and mix. Gather the mixture into a ball using your hands, adding a little extra flour to bring it together if necessary (harissa varies from brand to brand, so you may need to add a little more flour if your dough is sticky). Knead the dough in the bowl for a few minutes, ensuring you pull and stretch it to activate the gluten in the flour, which gives the finished pasta a nice smooth texture. Put the dough into a clean bowl, cover with plastic wrap, and refrigerate for 30 minutes.

Set your pasta machine on a clean work surface and dust the rollers with "00" flour. Using a rolling pin, flatten the dough a little so that it will fit into the rollers of the pasta machine. Push the dough through the pasta first on the thickest setting, then repeat, each time on a thinner setting down to setting number 3 (any lower and the dough may stick). Once the pasta sheet is nice and thin, select your preferred setting for either tagliatelle, linguine, or spaghetti, then pass the pasta through once more to cut it into your chosen pasta shape.

To cook, bring a pan of salted water to a boil, add the pasta, and cook for 2 to 3 minutes, or until al dente. Serve immediately with whatever you fancy.

LEMON & CUMIN PASTA DOUGH

I like to serve this pasta with crumbled feta and a healthy sprinkling of red chile flakes. This is heaven to me.

1½ cups "00" flour, plus extra for
    dusting
2 eggs
1 teaspoon cumin seeds, toasted and
    finely ground
finely grated zest of 1 unwaxed lemon
½ small packet (about ½oz) of fresh
    cilantro, leaves very finely chopped
good pinch of sea salt flakes
½ teaspoon freshly ground black pepper

SERVES 2 TO 4

Put all the ingredients into a large bowl and mix. Gather the mixture into a ball using your hands, adding a little extra flour to bring it together if necessary. Knead the dough in the bowl for a few minutes, ensuring you pull and stretch it to activate the gluten in the flour, which gives the finished pasta a nice smooth texture. Put the dough into a clean bowl, cover with plastic wrap, and refrigerate for 30 minutes.

Follow the method above to roll out and cook the pasta.

This pasta also works well with freshly cooked vegetables such as broccoli, peas, chard, or spinach leaves.

EGGPLANT IN TOMATO & TAMARIND SAUCE

Eggplant seems to be the Middle East's most popular vegetable, and for me it can sometimes be tricky to come up with new and interesting ways of using it. This simple eggplant dish is almost a stew, and the delicious sauce is really comforting. Cooking it slowly concentrates the flavors, so start preparing your sauce as early as possible to make this dish special. While I am happy to eat it by itself, you can serve it with basmati rice or bread and maybe even a few halves of hard-boiled egg.

vegetable oil

2 large onions, halved and thinly sliced
    into half-moons

1 garlic bulb, cloves peeled

1 teaspoon ground cinnamon

3 tablespoons thick unsweetened
    tamarind paste

2 x 14oz cans diced tomatoes

¼ cup honey

6 eggplants

Maldon sea salt flakes and freshly
    ground black pepper

SERVES 4 TO 6

Add enough vegetable oil to coat the bottom of a large saucepan and set over medium heat. Fry the onion for 8 to 10 minutes, or until browned but not burnt.

Add the garlic cloves to the saucepan along with the cinnamon and cook for a couple of minutes, until the garlic begins to soften. Stir in the tamarind paste, diced tomatoes, and honey and season generously. Reduce the heat to low and simmer gently for 1 hour (or more), until the sauce is reduced a little, and has sweetened and intensified in flavor.

Meanwhile, cut each eggplant in half lengthwise and remove the stem. Then slice each piece lengthwise into 4 wedges. Line a baking pan with a double layer of paper towels.

Pour enough vegetable oil into another large saucepan to fill to a depth of about 1 inch. Heat the oil over high heat, then add the eggplant wedges. Fry for 15 minutes, turning occasionally, until browned and cooked through. Remove with a slotted spoon and transfer to the prepared baking pan to drain. Pat with paper towels to absorb the excess oil.

Once the sauce is cooked, add the eggplant wedges to the sauce and carefully stir to ensure they are well coated. Heat through, then serve.

STUFFED ZUCCHINI
WITH PRESERVED LEMON, PINE NUTS & FETA

There is so much that can be done with zucchini, and this is a great way to use them for something a bit more substantial. Stuffing them with a bulgur-wheat filling spiked with flavorings complements the zucchini flesh beautifully. Serve them whole, or cut them into smaller portions if you have created a feast of several dishes.

½ cup bulgur wheat

4 large zucchini, halved lengthwise

4 fat preserved lemons, finely chopped

1 small pack (1oz) of flat-leaf parsley, finely chopped

⅓ cup pine nuts

7oz feta cheese, crumbled

1 teaspoon dried wild oregano

1 tablespoon garlic granules

finely grated zest of 1 unwaxed lemon

Maldon sea salt flakes and freshly ground black pepper

SERVES 4

Cook the bulgur wheat following the package directions, then drain and rinse it in cold water. Let drain until it is as dry as possible.

Preheat the oven to 475°F. Line a large baking pan with nonstick parchment paper.

Using a teaspoon, scoop all the flesh out of the zucchini halves, being careful not to break the skins. Arrange the skins on the prepared baking pan. Finely chop the zucchini flesh and put it into a large mixing bowl.

Add the preserved lemon, parsley, pine nuts, feta, oregano, garlic granules, and lemon zest to the zucchini flesh. Season with a little salt and a lot of pepper, then use your hands to mix until everything is well combined and the mixture feels moist. Divide the mixture into 8 portions. Heap one portion into one zucchini skin and press down on the filling mixture to really pack it in and fill the cavity. Repeat with the remaining portions of filling and zucchini skins.

Bake for 20 to 25 minutes, or until the skins are soft and the filling mixture is cooked through and browning on top. Serve immediately.

VEGETABLE DOLMA
WITH FREEKEH, PINE NUTS & POMEGRANATE MOLASSES

One of my favorite things to eat in the world is dolma. This recipe has a delicious sweet-and-sour flavor that reminds me of my childhood. They freeze well once cooked, so you can make them in large batches.

1 large onion

6 to 8 large white cabbage leaves (as intact as possible)

3 peppers (any color you like)

4 to 6 large vine tomatoes

olive oil

For the filling
vegetable oil

1 onion, finely chopped

1 teaspoon ground coriander

1 teaspoon ground cumin

1 teaspoon ground cinnamon

1 teaspoon dried red chile flakes (optional)

14oz can diced tomatoes

1 small pack (about 1oz) of flat-leaf parsley, finely chopped

1 cup freekeh

½ cup pine nuts

3 tablespoons pomegranate molasses

Maldon sea salt flakes and freshly ground black pepper

For the poaching liquid
1 cup boiling water

3 tablespoons pomegranate molasses

¼ cup superfine sugar

SERVES 4 TO 6

Preheat the oven to 400°F.

First prepare the vegetables for stuffing. Heat a large saucepan over high heat and half fill with boiling water. Make a single cut in the onion lengthwise, as if cutting it in half, but stop when you reach the center. Boil the cabbage leaves together with the whole onion for about 7 minutes, or until just starting to soften. Drain, then set aside until cool enough to handle. Carefully peel away the outer layers of the onion, keeping them intact (the cut you made earlier will help you remove the layers). Reserve the largest 4 to 6 layers for stuffing, then chop up the remaining onion and set it aside. Take the cooked cabbage leaves and cut out and discard the stalk from each leaf. Carefully slice the tops off of the peppers to create a lid for each pepper, then remove the seeds. Repeat the process with the tomatoes, but set aside the pulp and seeds to add to the filling.

Heat a drizzle of vegetable oil in a large skillet set over medium heat. Add the chopped onion and cook for 6 to 8 minutes, or until soft and beginning to turn golden. Stir in the reserved tomato pulp and seeds, the ground spices, and the red chile flakes and stir-fry for 1 to 2 minutes. Now mix in the diced tomatoes and parsley. Season the mixture well with salt and pepper, then cook for a further couple of minutes. Remove the pan from heat. Let the mixture cool a little, then add the freekeh, pine nuts, and pomegranate molasses and mix well.

Stuff the peppers and tomatoes with the filling mixture, leaving a gap between the filling and the lids to allow the filling mixture to expand during cooking, then stand them carefully in a large ovenproof dish. Divide the remaining filling mixture between the cabbage leaves and onion shells. Simply wrap and seal each cabbage leaf over the filling as best you can, and roll the onion around the filling as tightly as possible. Lay the stuffed onion and cabbage leaves in the dish.

Combine the ingredients for the poaching liquid in a small pitcher and stir until the sugar dissolves. Pour the liquid into the dish, then drizzle each dolma generously with olive oil. Roast for 45 to 55 minutes, or until nicely browned. Let cool and serve at room temperature.

HARISSA BLACK BEAN RAGOUT
WITH BUTTERNUT SQUASH

OK, so this dish isn't all that handsome, but you should never judge a book by its cover. I could happily eat this for breakfast, lunch, or dinner. Pile it onto toasted bread, top off with an egg, or just ladle it into a bowl and serve with a nice hunk of toasted bread: pure comfort.

olive oil

2 large onions, coarsely chopped

2 teaspoons garlic granules

2 teaspoons ground cumin

1 teaspoon ground cinnamon

1½ cups dried black beans

1½ quarts boiling water, divided

1¾lb butternut squash, peeled, seeded, and cut into coarse 1-inch chunks

2 tablespoons rose harissa, plus extra to serve

Maldon sea salt flakes and freshly ground black pepper

Greek yogurt, to serve

SERVES 4 TO 6

Heat a large saucepan over medium-low heat and add enough olive oil to coat the bottom of the pan. Add the onion and cook for about 6 to 8 minutes, or until soft and translucent, without browning.

Add the garlic granules and spices, then stir in the beans, adding a little extra oil if you feel you need more to coat the beans, and cook for about 5 minutes, stirring regularly. Then season generously with salt and pepper.

Pour 1 quart of the boiling water into the saucepan and stir well. Reduce the heat to medium-low and simmer gently for 25 to 30 minutes.

Mix in the butternut squash pieces (adding them at this stage will make them pleasingly dark in color when cooked), rose harissa, and the remaining boiling water. Taste and adjust the seasoning if desired, then cook for a further 30 minutes, or until the butternut squash is cooked through. Stir a little harissa through some Greek yogurt and serve with the ragout.

PAN-BAKED VEGETABLES

Who doesn't love the ease and convenience of a pan-baked vegetables? Chuck them all in, roast them, and you're done. Some of the best things I've eaten were born out of ease and convenience, and this is one of those super-lazy, feed-everyone type of creations. A nice piece of goat cheese with some great bread and a little salad on the side and I couldn't be happier.

1 eggplant, cut diagonally into
    slices ¼ inch thick

1 large zucchini, cut diagonally into slices
    ½ inch thick

1 red pepper, cored, seeded, and cut
    lengthwise into 6 strips

1 yellow pepper, cored, seeded, and cut
    lengthwise into 6 strips

2 potatoes (unpeeled), cut into
    slices ¼ inch thick

1 tablespoon dried wild oregano

1 tablespoon garlic granules

1 tablespoon cumin seeds

1 tablespoon dried red chile flakes
    (optional)

⅓ cup olive oil

Maldon sea salt flakes and freshly
    ground black pepper

SERVES 4

Preheat your oven to its highest setting. Line the largest baking pan you have with nonstick parchment paper.

Put the vegetables, herbs, and spices and the olive oil into a large mixing bowl, then season generously with salt and pepper. Use your hands to mix the vegetables until coated in the herbs, spices, and oil.

Tip the vegetables into the prepared pan and spread them out. It's fine if some of them overlap, but do what you can to expose as much of their surfaces as possible. Roast for 16 to 18 minutes, or until the vegetables are cooked through and browned. Serve immediately.

POTATO, RICOTTA & HERB DUMPLINGS
WITH WALNUTS & PUL BIBER BUTTER

For me, this is perhaps one of the most comforting recipes in this book. I love the combination of cheese and potato; add melted butter and a spike of chile heat and I'm in heaven. This recipe is inspired by a Transylvanian cheese and potato dumpling dish I once ate that has forever etched itself in my memory. Sadly, I never got the recipe, so I came up with this one instead.

For the dumplings
1lb 10oz potatoes
1lb 2oz ricotta cheese, drained well
2 eggs
1 small pack (about 1oz) of dill, finely chopped
½ cup "00" flour
light olive oil, for frying
Maldon sea salt flakes and freshly ground black pepper

For the sauce
½ cup salted butter
3 teaspoons pul biber chile flakes
½ cup chopped walnuts

SERVES 4 TO 6

Boil the potatoes whole for 25 to 35 minutes, or until cooked through. Drain and let cool slightly, peel, and then mash them in a large mixing bowl while they are still warm. Let cool.

Once the mashed potatoes have cooled, add the ricotta, eggs, dill, and flour and season generously with salt and pepper. Mix until evenly combined, then refrigerate for 30 minutes to firm up.

Shape the mixture into small dumplings a little larger than the size of your thumb. Dust each dumpling lightly with the flour and flatten slightly. Heat a skillet over medium-high heat and add a drizzle of light olive oil. Flash-fry the dumplings for just a few minutes—the outsides should be golden brown and the centers just warmed through.

To make sauce, melt the butter in a small saucepan over low heat and stir in the pul biber and walnuts.

Once the butter is warm, transfer the dumplings to a warmed serving plate, drizzle with the pul biber and walnut butter, and serve immediately.

CUPBOARD
SUSTENANCE

FETA, PUL BIBER & OREGANO MACARONI BAKE

I have so much love for "mac and cheese" of every description. From the simple classic to the meaty Cypriot pastitsio, it's all good to me. This version was something I came up with for my neighbor Janet who just loves macaroni and cheese, and also enjoys spicy flavors, and not surprisingly, it is absolutely delicious and extremely comforting, too.

3¼ cups macaroni

2 heaped teaspoons pul biber chile flakes

handful of oregano leaves, coarsely chopped

finely grated zest of 1 unwaxed lemon

For the sauce

½ cup all-purpose flour

3½ tablespoons salted butter

2 cups whole milk

½ cup crème fraîche

14oz feta cheese, crumbled (reserve a handful for the topping)

1 egg, beaten

2 teaspoons freshly ground black pepper

Maldon sea salt flakes

SERVES 6 TO 8

First make the feta sauce. Heat a large saucepan over medium-low heat. Add the flour and dry-toast for 1 minute, stirring constantly and bashing out any lumps with a wooden spoon. Add the butter and stir in the milk and crème fraîche, then whisk until the butter has melted, the milk is incorporated, and the mixture is smooth. Add the feta and stir in, then remove from the heat and quickly stir in the beaten egg, the pepper, and add a sprinkling of salt (bear in mind that the feta will be salty).

Preheat the oven to 425°F. Select a large baking pan or ovenproof dish about 10½ x 8 inches in size.

Boil the macaroni following the package directions, then drain the pasta and return it to the pan. Add the pul biber, oregano, lemon zest, and feta sauce and stir well. Transfer the mixture to the baking pan or dish, then crumble the reserved feta evenly over the surface. Bake for 25 minutes, or until browning on top. Serve immediately.

LEMON, BLACK PEPPER, PECORINO & CABBAGE RICE

This is a controversial version of a risotto using basmati, which is a method I first spotted in a Gérard Depardieu cookbook many years ago. I won't say it is a better rice to use for making risotto, but I will say that I always have it in the house, so for me it is a convenient twist. I have taken my love of spaghetti cacio e pepe (with Pecorino and black pepper) as inspiration for this recipe, adding fresh lemon zest. There are also lovely ribbons of delicate cabbage leaves, which I think complement the rich, cheesy sauce perfectly.

olive oil

1 white onion, very finely chopped

1½ cups basmati rice

½ cup butter, divided

1¼ to 1½ quarts boiling water

1 teaspoon freshly ground black pepper
   (mill it coarsely)

3½oz pecorino cheese, finely grated,
   plus extra (optional) to serve

½ large Savoy cabbage, shredded
   into ribbons

finely grated zest of 1 unwaxed lemon

SERVES 4 TO 6

Heat a large saucepan over medium-low heat and add enough olive oil to coat the bottom of the pan. Add the onion and cook for about 8 to 10 minutes, or until soft and translucent, without browning.

Add the rice and half the butter to the saucepan and stir gently for a minute or so. Then begin adding the boiling water a ladleful at a time, stirring constantly, ensuring that each ladleful of water is absorbed before adding the next. Don't be tempted to increase the heat to speed up the process—you don't want the liquid to evaporate too quickly, otherwise the rice won't cook properly. Once you have used one-third of the water, check the rice to see if it has cooked through (the grains should not be hard in the center). Continue stirring and adding water this way until the rice is cooked to your liking.

Add the pepper and pecorino and stir rapidly to ensure the mixture becomes creamy and smooth. Now stir in the cabbage, followed by the remaining butter. Lastly, mix in the lemon zest. Take the pan off the heat and ladle the risotto into serving bowls. Drizzle each serving with a little olive oil, then scatter with some pecorino, if desired. Serve immediately.

HARISSA & SOBA NOODLE SALAD

WITH BROCCOLI, SESAME & NIGELLA SEEDS

The first time I tried Nigella Lawson's soba noodle salad, I fell head over heels in love with it. Although this version bears little similarity to the original, it remains a polite and respectful nod to the ever-inspiring Ms. Lawson and her wonderful soba noodle salad, with the addition of a few Sabrina staples.

9oz soba noodles

olive oil

10½oz broccolini, halved lengthwise

⅓ cup sesame seeds, toasted

1½ tablespoons nigella seeds

For the dressing

2 tablespoons rose harissa

3 tablespoons tahini

1 fat garlic clove, crushed

juice of ½ lime

2 tablespoons honey

approximately ⅓ cup lukewarm water

SERVES 4 TO 6

Cook the soba noodles following the package directions, then drain and rinse them under cold running water. Drain again, then set aside.

Heat a drizzle of olive oil in a skillet over medium-high heat. Rinse the broccoli stalks and florets, drain them briefly, then add them to the pan along with the residual water from rinsing. Sauté for a couple of minutes, stirring, then cover the pan with a lid and steam for 2 to 3 minutes. Remove the broccoli from the pan and set aside to cool.

Mix the ingredients for the dressing together in a bowl, adding only as much of the lukewarm water as you need (the sauce should be just runny enough to coat all the noodles).

Put the noodles into a large mixing bowl. Pour over the dressing, then add the sesame and nigella seeds and the broccoli, and toss well. Serve immediately.

ROASTED EGGPLANT & CARROT COUSCOUS
WITH PRESERVED LEMON

To all those people who say that couscous is bland, I say you just haven't tried the right recipe yet. Couscous should be used as a carrier for bold flavors, so if you're wondering what to do with a package of it, try raiding your spice rack and store cupboard in search of strong flavors that will give character to your couscous-based meals. This tasty dish is delicious served either hot or cold, which means any leftovers are ideal for tomorrow's lunch boxes.

4 eggplants, cut into 1-inch dice

extra virgin olive oil

6 small carrots, peeled and cut into batons

2 teaspoons dried wild oregano

2 teaspoons cumin seeds

1⅔ cups couscous

2 teaspoons turmeric

1 teaspoon ground cinnamon

2 teaspoons ground coriander

2 fat garlic cloves, crushed

2 cups hot water

4 to 5 preserved lemons, seeded and finely chopped

1 small pack (about 1oz) of dill, finely chopped

1 small pack (about 1oz) of flat-leaf parsley, finely chopped

Maldon sea salt flakes and freshly ground black pepper

SERVES 6 TO 8

Preheat the oven to 425°F. Line the largest baking pan you have, plus another baking pan, with nonstick parchment paper.

Put the eggplant cubes into the largest prepared pan, season with pepper, drizzle with a generous amount of olive oil, and place the pan on the higher rack in the oven. Put the carrots into the other pan, season with salt, pepper, and the oregano and drizzle with olive oil. Add to the oven to roast for 25 to 30 minutes, until the eggplant is cooked through and browned, and the carrots are cooked and charred around the edges.

Toast the cumin seeds in a large, dry saucepan over medium-high heat for 1 minute, then take the pan off the heat, add the couscous, and allow it to toast briefly. Stir in the other spices, the crushed garlic, and measured hot water with a generous amount of salt and pepper. Cover the saucepan with a lid (or use plastic wrap) and set aside for 8 to 10 minutes to allow the couscous grains to absorb the liquid.

Once the liquid has been absorbed, use a fork to carefully fluff up the couscous. Now add the roasted eggplants and carrots, the preserved lemon, and fresh herbs and fold them in carefully. Return to the heat briefly, if needed, and serve hot.

FREEKEH, PEA, FETA & SCALLION FRITTERS

Freekeh is wheat that is harvested while still young and green, smoked, and sometimes broken. So flavorsome, its somewhat grassy and nutty taste is delicious in salads, soups, pilafs, and more. Here, I capitalize on its smoky flavor and chewy texture and combine it with the humble pea and some creamy, salty feta to make these wonderfully crisp and moreish fritters. A little yogurt on the side is a lovely addition.

vegetable oil, for frying

¾ cup freekeh, boiled for 25 minutes, rinsed, and drained until dry

5 scallions, thinly sliced from root to tip

⅔ cup fresh peas

7oz feta cheese, crumbled

1 tablespoon dried wild thyme

1 tablespoon pul biber chile flakes

2 large eggs

⅓ cup all-purpose flour

Maldon sea salt flakes and freshly ground black pepper

Greek yogurt, to serve

MAKES 12 TO 16

Pour enough vegetable oil into a large, deep skillet or saucepan to fill to a depth of about 2 inches. Heat the oil over medium-high heat and bring to frying temperature (add a pinch of mixture; if it sizzles immediately, the oil is hot enough). Line a baking pan with a double layer of paper towels.

Combine the remaining ingredients in a large mixing bowl, seasoning well with salt and pepper. Mix using your hands for a few minutes until the mixture becomes easier to work.

When the oil is ready for frying, use 2 tablespoons to form quenelles of the mixture: scoop up the mixture with one spoon and use the other to press down on the mixture to shape and compress it. Carefully lower the quenelles into the hot oil one at a time, as you make them, and fry in batches, for 3 to 4 minutes, or until deep golden brown all over. Remove the fritters from the oil with a slotted spoon and transfer to the prepared plate to drain. Sprinkle with salt flakes and serve immediately with Greek yogurt for dipping.

PEA, DILL & GARLIC RICE
WITH SAFFRON

This is my twist on the Persian classic baghala polow, a lovely aromatic dill and fava bean rice dish. This version uses simple, cost-effective, and readily available frozen peas and I am very pleased with the results. The best news? No fiddly peeling of pods is necessary.

1¾ cups basmati rice

vegetable oil

1 large garlic bulb, cloves peeled and
   thinly sliced

generous pinch of saffron threads

2 cups finely chopped dill

½ cup butter, cubed

2½ cups frozen peas

Maldon sea salt flakes and freshly
   ground black pepper

SERVES 6 TO 8

Cook the rice following the package directions. Once cooked, drain and rinse under cold running water. Drain again, then set aside.

Heat a drizzle of vegetable oil in a large saucepan over medium-low heat. Add the garlic and fry for 1 to 2 minutes, or until soft and translucent and beginning to turn golden around the edges.

Crumble in the saffron, breaking it down as much as possible, stir well, then add the dill and fry for a few minutes more, until the dill wilts. Season heavily with salt and pepper (add enough at this stage to season the peas and all the cooked rice) and mix well.

Stir the butter into the pan, allow it to melt, then add the cooked rice. Stir-fry for 2 to 3 minutes, then add the peas and cook for a few more minutes. Cover the pan with a lid and cook for a final 10 to 15 minutes. Taste and adjust the seasoning if necessary before serving.

SPICED GREEN BEAN & TOMATO RICE

I confess that I have done something no respectable Iranian should ever do: extract the meat from a much-loved Persian recipe classic, loobia polow (rice cooked with green beans and meat). But I am pleased to report that it is every bit as good as the original. We Iranians tend to embrace meat in everything, but the truth is that this vegetarian version has plenty going for it.

2 cups basmati rice

¼ to ⅓ cup ghee or vegetable oil, divided

1 large onion, finely chopped

14oz fine green beans, trimmed, each cut into 4 equal pieces

4 fat garlic cloves, thinly sliced

1 teaspoon turmeric

2 teaspoons ground cinnamon

¼ cup tomato paste

⅓ cup butter, cubed

1 tablespoon Greek yogurt

pinch of good-quality saffron threads, ground to a powder using a mortar and pestle, then steeped in 2 to 3 tablespoons boiling water until cool

Maldon sea salt flakes and freshly ground black pepper

SERVES 4 TO 6

Bring a saucepan of water to a boil, add the rice, and parboil for 6 minutes. Once parboiled, drain the rice in a sieve and rinse thoroughly under cold running water for a couple of minutes, using your fingers to wash off the starch. Shake vigorously to drain, then set aside.

Heat 2 tablespoons of the ghee or vegetable oil in a large skillet over medium heat. Add the onion and cook for 6 to 8 minutes, or until soft and translucent. Add the green beans, stir well, and cook for 15 to 20 minutes, or until they are completely soft. Add the garlic and cook for a further 10 to 15 minutes. Mix in the turmeric and cinnamon, and season heavily with salt and pepper (be very generous, as this will need to season all the cooked rice, too). Once the garlic has softened, stir in the tomato paste and cook for 5 minutes. Stir in the butter, then take the pan off the heat. Tip the rice into the green bean mixture and fold everything together gently, without breaking the rice grains, until evenly combined.

Select a large lidded saucepan and line the inside bottom with a disk of nonstick parchment paper cut slightly larger than the bottom itself. Heat the pan over low heat, add the remaining ghee or oil, and allow it to melt over the paper. Stir the yogurt into the saffron solution, then add it to the melted ghee or oil and stir in quickly.

Scatter the green bean and rice mixture into the saucepan, pressing it into the edges and bottom of the pan to create a flat bottom. Smooth the surface, then, using the handle of a wooden spoon, poke a series of holes into the rice, piercing all the way to the bottom of the pan (this allows the steam to circulate). Wrap the pan lid in a dishcloth, cover the pan with the lid, and cook on the lowest temperature for 45 minutes.

Once cooked, remove the lid and place a large platter over the saucepan. Carefully flip the rice onto the platter to reveal the crunchy *tahdig* base. If it doesn't turn out perfectly, remove the crunchy base, slice it into portions and place it over the rice, as pictured.

MUSHROOM, TAHINI & HARISSA SPAGHETTI

In this dish the mushrooms are blitzed to a consistency similar to ground beef, so it's easy to forget they are the key ingredient. This full-bodied, gratifying noodle dish draws inspiration from the dan dan noodles of the Sichuan province of China. You can make it as a dry noodle dish, or simply add water or milk to make it more of a soup.

handful of sesame seeds

½ teaspoon dried red chile flakes

2¼lb cremino mushrooms

olive oil

6 fat garlic cloves, thinly sliced

1 heaped teaspoon ground cinnamon

2 teaspoons ground cumin

1 teaspoon coarsely ground black pepper

¼ cup light soy sauce, plus extra to taste

3 tablespoons rose harissa

2 tablespoons tahini

1 quart boiling water (or 2 cups boiling water and 2 cups milk)

14oz spaghetti or egg noodles, cooked following the package directions

1 bunch of scallions, thinly sliced diagonally from root to tip

1 small pack (about 1oz) of fresh cilantro, coarsely chopped

Maldon sea salt flakes

SERVES 4 TO 6

Toast the sesame seeds and red chile flakes in a small, dry skillet over medium heat for 2 to 3 minutes, or until they release their aroma. Remove from the heat and set aside.

Put the mushrooms into the bowl of a food processor and pulse until coarsely blitzed, ensuring not to overprocess them. Alternatively, chop the mushrooms finely by hand.

Heat a wok or large saucepan over high heat. Add the chopped mushrooms to the dry pan and fry for 5 to 6 minutes, or until they have released some moisture and are nicely browned. Add a drizzle of olive oil to the pan, reduce the heat to medium, then add the garlic and fry for 2 minutes, or until it is translucent.

Add the cinnamon, cumin, and pepper to the pan and fry for 2 minutes. Now mix in the soy sauce, harissa, and tahini. Stir in the boiling water as desired (and milk, if using), depending on whether you want just enough sauce to coat all the noodles, or more of a soup. Season with salt and extra soy sauce to taste, then increase the heat and bring to a boil. Stir in the cooked noodles, scallion, and cilantro, and as soon as the noodles have heated through, serve with the toasted sesame seeds and dried red chile flakes sprinkled on top.

SPAGHETTI WITH OLIVES, BROCCOLI & FETA

I am obsessed with adding greens to pasta dishes. Broccoli and cabbage are usually my favorites, and both work well in this recipe. I always keep feta in my refrigerator, and usually have olives of some description in a corner of my cupboard, both of which are great to throw into a tangle of pasta to add a tangy bite of flavor. It doesn't really matter which type of pasta you use. I grab whatever I have handy. I always make a big batch of this dish, and sometimes I end up eating leftovers cold for breakfast, but that really is another story.

olive oil

1 large garlic bulb, cloves peeled and
 thinly sliced

1lb 2oz spaghetti or linguine

10½oz broccoli, cut into florets

1 cup pitted black olives or mixed olives,
 halved or coarsely chopped

2 to 3 tablespoons pul biber chile flakes

finely grated zest of 2 unwaxed lemons

14oz feta cheese, crumbled

Maldon sea salt flakes and freshly ground
 black pepper

SERVES 4 TO 6

Bring a large saucepan of generously salted water to a boil over high heat.

Meanwhile, place another large saucepan over medium-low heat and add enough olive oil to coat the bottom of the pan. Add the garlic and cook for about 6 to 8 minutes, or until soft and translucent, without browning. Remove from the heat.

Add the pasta to the boiling water and cook following the package directions. Once half the cooking time for the pasta has elapsed, set the pan containing the garlic back on the stove over medium-high heat and add the broccoli. Stir-fry for the few remaining minutes needed to cook the pasta.

Using tongs, lift the pasta from the water and add it to the broccoli pan along with a few spoonfuls of the pasta cooking water. Stir well, then add a good drizzle of olive oil and a generous seasoning of salt and black pepper. Add the olives, pul biber chile flakes, and lemon zest and combine. Then add the feta and toss the pasta well to evenly distribute the ingredients. If the dish seems a little dry, stir in some more of the pasta water. Serve immediately.

SPECTACULAR SIDES

SHALLOT BLOSSOMS
WITH PAPRIKA CRÈME FRAÎCHE

I first tried a version of these at a restaurant on vacation in the States many moons ago. We loved them so much, we ordered plate after plate! My version here is every bit as delicious, and can be served as finger food or as a nice addition to a meal. The dip is a simple yet perfect accompaniment.

vegetable oil, for frying

1lb long shallots, peeled but
    kept whole

¾ cup all-purpose flour

1 tablespoon paprika

1 tablespoon garlic granules

1 tablespoon dried wild oregano

2 teaspoons celery salt

1 teaspoon cayenne pepper

1 large egg, beaten

For the dip

1 cup crème fraîche

2 teaspoons paprika

Maldon sea salt flakes and freshly
    ground black pepper

SERVES 4

To make the dip, mix the crème fraîche and paprika in a bowl and season with a generous amount of salt and pepper. Refrigerate until ready to serve.

Pour enough vegetable oil into a large deep skillet or saucepan to fill to a depth of about 2 inches. Heat the oil over medium-high heat and bring to frying temperature (add a pinch of the batter mixture; if it sizzles immediately, the oil is hot enough). Line a plate with a double layer of paper towels.

Meanwhile, cut the root off of the shallots. Cutting through the root end toward the tip, make about 8 cuts into each shallot to create matchstick-sized "petals," stopping ½ inch from the tip so that the shallot stays intact. Gently separate out the cut ends of each shallot.

Put the flour, paprika, garlic granules, celery salt, and cayenne pepper into a deep plastic container and mix well. Put the beaten egg into a separate bowl.

When the oil is at frying temperature, dip a shallot into the spiced flour and shake it around to coat all the edges in the flour. Shake off any excess flour, then dip it immediately into the beaten egg, again doing your best to coat the insides. Shake off any excess egg, then return the shallot to the spiced flour and coat a second time in the flour. Carefully lower the coated shallot into the hot oil. Repeat with the remaining shallots. Fry for 2 to 3 minutes, turning halfway, until all sides are deep golden brown. Remove from the oil using a slotted spoon and transfer to the prepared plate to drain. Serve hot, sprinkled with extra salt flakes and with the dip on the side.

CRUMBED ASPARAGUS

WITH SAFFRON YOGURT

The closest thing I've ever had to this dish was asparagus tempura, and I remember thinking what a complete joy it was. This version is crumbed instead of battered, which helps retain a wonderful texture. The saffron yogurt is my version of an aioli but, of course, Middle Eastern style.

vegetable oil, for frying

1 large egg, beaten

1 heaped tablespoon garlic granules

¾ cup fine white bread crumbs

5½oz asparagus spears, woody ends trimmed off

Maldon sea salt flakes and freshly ground black pepper

For the saffron yogurt

pinch of saffron threads, ground to a powder using a mortar and pestle

1 tablespoon boiling water

1 cup Greek yogurt

1 small garlic clove (or ½ fat one), crushed

Maldon sea salt flakes and freshly ground black pepper

SERVES 4

To make the saffron yogurt, put the saffron threads into a small cup and pour in the measured boiling water. Gently swirl the mixture and then let steep until the liquid is cool. Stir the saffron solution into the Greek yogurt, add the garlic and a generous amount of salt and pepper, and mix well. Refrigerate until ready to serve.

Pour enough vegetable oil into a large, deep skillet or saucepan to fill to a depth of about 2 inches. Heat the oil over medium-high heat and bring to frying temperature (add a pinch of the bread crumb mixture; if it sizzles immediately, the oil is hot enough). Line a plate with a double layer of paper towels.

Meanwhile, put the beaten egg, garlic granules, and a generous amount of salt and pepper into a shallow bowl and stir well until the mixture is as smooth as possible. Put the bread crumbs on a plate.

When the oil is at frying temperature, dip an asparagus spear into the beaten egg to coat, then roll it in the bread crumbs. Now immediately lower the breaded asparagus carefully into the hot oil and fry for a few minutes, until golden brown all over. Repeat with the remaining asparagus, but do not overcrowd the pan (fry in batches if necessary). Remove the asparagus carefully using a slotted spoon or long-handled tongs and transfer to the prepared plate to drain. Serve hot, sprinkled with extra salt flakes and with the saffron yogurt on the side.

CHARGRILLED SCALLIONS
WITH HAZELNUTS & LIME & HONEY DRESSING

I love scallions in everything, on everything, and with everything. Traditionally we eat them raw with bread and feta cheese as staple fare of the Persian table. Grilling them mellows out the oniony flavor, and intense charring works beautifully with the sweetness of cooked onion flesh. Chargrilling them on a barbecue is ideal, but you can also cook them easily using a ridged grill pan on the stove. The dressing for this delicious salad combines well with the grilled onion, and the toasted hazelnuts add a satisfying crunch. This dish is great served alone or as an accompaniment at any time of year.

¼ cup blanched hazelnuts

12 scallions

For the dressing

1½ tablespoons olive oil

juice of ½ fat lime

1 tablespoon honey

Maldon sea salt flakes and freshly
    ground black pepper

To garnish

2 pinches of pul biber chile flakes

finely grated zest of ½ unwaxed lime

SERVES 4 TO 6

First make the dressing. Combine the olive oil, lime juice, honey, and a good amount of salt and pepper in a small bowl and set aside.

Toast the hazelnuts in a dry skillet set over medium-high heat until charred but not burnt. Set aside until cool enough to handle, then coarsely halve or chop them.

Meanwhile, bring some water to a boil in a saucepan. Blanch the scallions in the boiling water for 2 minutes, then drain and dry them well with paper towels. Meanwhile, preheat a ridged grill pan over high heat. Arrange the blanched scallions on the grill pan and chargrill for a few minutes on each side, until char marks appear.

Arrange the scallions on a serving plate and scatter with the hazelnuts, then drizzle with the dressing. Sprinkle with the pul biber chile flakes and grated lime zest, then serve.

STIR-FRIED CAVOLO NERO, CHESTNUTS, MUSHROOMS & CHICKPEAS

I first made this warm salad back in my supperclub days, when I had an unannounced vegan guest. Thankfully, a well-stocked refrigerator and a can of chickpeas proved to be my savior. My guest loved this dish so much, I began serving it regularly as an autumnal vegan offering. It really is quite delicious.

1lb 2oz cremino mushrooms, chopped

2 tablespoons garlic oil

1 teaspoon ground cumin

½ teaspoon turmeric

½ teaspoon ground cinnamon

½ teaspoon cayenne pepper

generous pinch of Maldon sea salt flakes

9oz cavolo nero, tough stalks discarded, coarsely chopped

10 to 12 vacuum-packed cooked chestnuts, halved

14oz can chickpeas, drained and rinsed

SERVES 4 TO 6

Heat a large saucepan over high heat until hot, then add the mushrooms to the dry pan and cook for 6 to 8 minutes, stirring a couple of times only, until any moisture has evaporated. Reduce the heat, then add the garlic oil, spices, and salt.

Add the cavolo nero to the saucepan and stir-fry for 1 minute, then mix in the halved chestnuts and chickpeas and cook for another couple of minutes, until the cavolo nero has wilted and is cooked (it should retain some bite). Serve immediately.

BUTTERNUT SQUASH MASHED WITH GARLIC & CHILE FLAKES

I don't think I have ever come across a butternut squash dish I didn't like. This is definitely one of my favorites. It makes a perfect side dish but, if I'm in the right mood, no one can stop me from devouring it on its own.

2 x 2¼lb butternut squashes (unpeeled)

olive oil

2 fat garlic cloves, crushed

1 teaspoon dried red chile flakes

generous walnut-sized lump of butter

2 tablespoons tahini

2 pinches of sumac

handful of pine nuts

Maldon sea salt flakes and freshly
    ground black pepper

SERVES 4 TO 6

Preheat the oven to 400°F.

Cut the butternut squashes in half lengthwise and scoop out and discard the seeds. Drizzle each squash half with olive oil and rub the oil all over them to coat. Place the squash halves on a baking pan and roast for 1 hour, or until the flesh is soft and cooked through.

Remove the roasted squash halves from the oven and set them on a cutting board. Use a spoon to scoop out the flesh and place it in a mixing bowl, discarding the skins. Add the garlic and red chile flakes and mash everything together until smooth, then add the butter and mix well. Transfer the mashed squash to a saucepan and set the pan over medium heat. Cook the squash for 5 minutes, stirring occasionally.

Transfer the mashed butternut squash to a large wide serving platter and spread it out to the edges of the dish. Drizzle with the tahini, sprinkle with the sumac, and scatter with the pine nuts. Finish with a drizzle of olive oil, and serve immediately.

BAKED CELERY ROOT & HARISSA

I have a strange love for the smell of cut raw celery root. Its subtle, citrusy notes send me into a frenzy. While we have the French to thank for the marvelous celery root remoulade, and we do occasionally use celery root to make purées, I think this is another of those greatly underused vegetables. With a little harissa magic, it makes for the most wonderful baked dish, its natural flavor standing up well against the spice of the harissa.

1lb 10oz celery root, peeled

2 tablespoons honey

2 tablespoons good-quality vegetable stock powder

2 tablespoons harissa

approximately 2 cups boiling water

SERVES 6 TO 8

Preheat the oven to 425°F. Select a round ovenproof dish approximately 8 inches in diameter.

Slice the celery root into 3 equally thick disks, then cut each disk in half. Thinly slice each piece. Arrange the sliced celery root in the dish.

Put the honey, stock, and harissa into a large measuring cup and add enough boiling water to bring the liquid level up to 14fl oz (1¾ cups). Stir well, then pour the mixture evenly over the celery root. Bake for 40 to 45 minutes, or until the celery root is cooked through. Halfway through the cooking time, use a spoon to baste the celery root and push it down into the sauce, then return the dish to the oven to finish cooking. Serve immediately.

ROASTED PARSNIPS

WITH HARISSA ORANGE GLAZE

Growing up in England has meant that parsnips have played an important role in our home cooking, and I couldn't imagine a Christmas meal without them. I like to roast them just with salt and pepper and dip them into horseradish cream, and I adore them in cakes, because their natural sweetness is really something special. This recipe is a sticky, chewy, spicy, sweet revelation. I challenge you not to eat half of it before it even hits the table!

2¼lb parsnips

olive oil

Maldon sea salt flakes and freshly
   ground black pepper

For the glaze

3 tablespoons honey

2 tablespoons rose harissa

finely grated zest and juice of
   1 unwaxed orange

SERVES 4 TO 6

Preheat the oven to 425°F. Line the largest roasting dish you have with nonstick parchment paper.

Mix the glaze ingredients together in a small bowl and set aside.

Peel the parsnips and cut them roughly into pieces 1 inch in thickness and about 2 inches long. Don't worry about being too precise; just make them all approximately the same size. Put them into the roasting dish, drizzle with olive oil, and season well with salt and pepper. Roast for 30 minutes, or until cooked through and slightly brown.

Pour the glaze over the parsnips, toss well to coat, and roast for a further 10 to 12 minutes. Remove the dish from the oven, stir the parsnip pieces in the glaze remaining in the roasting pan once more, and serve.

SPICED SWEET POTATO & ONION HASH

This kind of one-pan dish is literally my go-to recipe when I'm craving something simple but effective. If you wanted to make it any more satisfying, or bulk it up to serve two for brunch, then an egg on top—fried or poached—is the perfect pairing.

vegetable oil, for frying

2 large slices of sourdough bread, cut into rough cubes

1 small pack (about 1oz) of flat-leaf parsley, coarsely chopped

1lb 2oz sweet potatoes, peeled and cut into cubes

1 teaspoon black mustard seeds

2 teaspoons coriander seeds

1 onion, coarsely chopped

2 garlic cloves, bashed

Maldon sea salt flakes and freshly ground black pepper

SERVES 2 TO 4

Heat a skillet over medium heat and add a good drizzle of vegetable oil. Add the bread cubes, season generously with salt and pepper, and stir well. Cook for about 5 minutes, or until the bread is browned. Remove the pan from the heat, stir in the chopped parsley, and set aside.

Heat a separate large skillet over medium heat and drizzle in enough oil to generously coat the bottom of the pan. Add the sweet potato and cook, turning frequently, for 30 minutes or until the potato begins to soften.

Add the mustard and coriander seeds and the chopped onion to the pan and cook, stirring, for 1 minute, or until the seeds start to pop. Add the garlic and stir, ensuring everything is coated in the seeds. Cook for 1 to 2 minutes, or until the garlic has softened.

Tip the bread cubes into the pan with the sweet potato. Mix everything together, then serve.

TARUNIMA'S OKRA FRIES

My friend Tarunima makes the most gorgeous and delicious cakes I've ever tasted. And not only that, but pretty much everything she creates has so much flavor it's hard to control yourself when she's cooking for you. Her spiced okra fries may well be my favorite type of fries of all. Even though my recipe isn't exactly the same as Tarunima's, it is still pretty darn fantastic. If you haven't tried spiced okra fries, you really haven't lived!

vegetable oil, for frying

2 teaspoons garlic granules

1 heaped teaspoon chili powder

2 teaspoons turmeric

¼ cup chickpea (gram) flour

2 tablespoons cornstarch

¾ lb okra, each pod quartered lengthwise

Maldon sea salt flakes and freshly
    ground black pepper

SERVES 4 TO 6

Pour enough vegetable oil into a large, deep skillet or saucepan to fill to a depth of about 2 inches. Heat the oil over medium-high heat and bring to frying temperature (add a small piece of okra; if it sizzles immediately, the oil is hot enough). Line a plate with a double layer of paper towels.

Meanwhile, combine the garlic granules, spices, and flours in a large mixing bowl and season with salt and pepper. Add the okra and mix well to ensure the okra strips are well coated (add a few teaspoons of water if necessary to help the mixture stick to the okra). Using your hands, coat the okra all over in the mixture.

When the oil is ready for deep-frying, carefully lower the strips, a few at a time, into the oil. Do not overcrowd the pan, and cook in batches if necessary. Fry for about 6 to 8 minutes, until crisp and golden. Remove the okra fries using a slotted spoon and transfer to the prepared plate to drain. Sprinkle with salt flakes and serve immediately.

BAKED SWEET POTATO WITH COCONUT & THYME

Dauphinoise potatoes are one of my favorite things. This is a variation of that classic, employing Jamaican-inspired flavors found in rice and peas, and my love for sweet potatoes. I promise you, this dish is incredibly moreish.

1lb 10oz sweet potatoes, peeled

2 fat garlic cloves, thinly sliced

4 to 5 sprigs of thyme, leaves picked and coarsely chopped, reserving some for garnish

14oz can full-fat coconut milk

Maldon sea salt flakes and freshly ground black pepper

SERVES 6 TO 8

Preheat the oven to 425°F. Select a large baking pan or ovenproof dish about 10½ x 8 inches in size.

Thinly slice the sweet potatoes using a mandoline slicer, or with a food processor with the slicing attachment set to a medium thickness. Alternatively, thinly slice them with a knife.

Use one-quarter of the sweet potatoes to create an overlapping layer in the bottom of the baking pan or dish. Distribute one-third of the garlic and thyme over the potato layer and season generously with salt and pepper. Repeat this layering process, finishing with a layer of sweet potato slices. Pour the coconut milk evenly over the potatoes, then gently press down on the contents of the dish with a spatula to compress. Season with salt and pepper and sprinkle with the reserved thyme.

Bake for 20 minutes, then press down on the potato slices with the spatula to submerge them in the coconut milk. Return the dish to the oven and bake for a further 20 to 25 minutes. Serve immediately.

TEMPURA SCALLIONS
WITH HARISSA KETCHUP

You could coat a shoe in tempura batter and I'd probably love it. There is something endlessly satisfying about the ludicrously crunchy yet light coating, and it works beautifully with anything, from seafood to vegetables. For this dish I chose scallions; they are always available and their sweetness only intensifies when cooked. They're perfect with my sweet and spicy harissa ketchup dip on the side.

vegetable oil, for frying

12 scallions

For the harissa ketchup

½ cup tomato ketchup

2 tablespoons rose harissa

For the tempura batter

1 large egg

1 cup all-purpose flour

1 cup ice-cold water

ice cubes

SERVES 4 TO 6

Pour enough vegetable oil into a large, deep skillet or saucepan to fill to a depth of about 2 inches. Heat the oil over medium-high heat and bring to frying temperature (add a teaspoon of batter; if it sizzles immediately, the oil is hot enough). Line a plate with a double layer of paper towels.

To make the harissa ketchup, combine the ketchup and harissa in a bowl. Set aside.

Crack the egg into a large mixing bowl and add the flour, but do not mix together. Have your the iced water ready (add ice cubes to help keep it cold, but make sure they don't end up in the batter).

When the oil is ready for frying, pour the iced water into the bowl with the egg and flour and, using chopsticks or the handle of a wooden spoon (not a whisk), mix the flour, egg, and water together quickly, until most of the flour is dissolved. Ensure you don't overbeat the mixture.

Dip the scallions, one at a time, into the batter to coat them well, then immediately (and carefully) transfer to the hot oil. Fry in batches for 2 to 3 minutes, until the batter is crisp (it won't turn brown). Using a slotted spoon or long-handled tongs, remove the scallions, shake off the excess oil, and transfer to the prepared plate to drain. Sprinkle with salt flakes and serve immediately with the harissa ketchup.

KAFFIR LIME & SPICE-ROASTED CHICKPEAS

I'm a nibbler and a picker. If you leave little plates of food in front of me, I will happily graze on them instead of having a proper meal. This dish is packed full of flavor and great served hot or cold, alone or tossed into a salad of any kind to add more dimension. As I've always maintained, feta makes everything better, so a little crumbled feta cheese would be a heavenly addition, but is by no means necessary.

2 x 14oz cans chickpeas, drained

1 teaspoon medium curry powder

1 teaspoon paprika

1 teaspoon turmeric

1 teaspoon ground cinnamon

1 teaspoon ground cumin

8 kaffir lime leaves

1 teaspoon ground fenugreek

2 teaspoons dried mint

2 fat garlic cloves, crushed

juice of ½ fat lime

2 tablespoons olive oil

generous amount of Maldon sea salt
    flakes and freshly ground black pepper

SERVES 4 TO 6

Preheat oven to 425°F. Line a baking pan with nonstick parchment paper.

Put all the ingredients into a large mixing bowl and mix well, ensuring the chickpeas are well coated in the spiced oil. Tip the mixture into the prepared pan and roast for 20 minutes, stirring and turning the chickpeas over once halfway through the cooking time. Serve immediately.

ROASTED NEW POTATOES WITH SPICED CITRUS BUTTER

This is a simple way of adding a kick of flavor to roasted new potatoes (it works brilliantly with many other vegetables, too). Essentially, the magic comes from the spiced butter, which contains sumac. You'll be surprised at the versatility of sumac, and hopefully this recipe shows you one more way in which to use this mild citrusy spice.

1lb 10oz new potatoes (unpeeled), halved lengthwise

olive oil

Maldon sea salt flakes and freshly ground black pepper

For the spiced butter

3½ tablespoons salted butter, softened

2 teaspoons sumac

finely grated zest of 1 unwaxed orange

finely grated zest of 1 unwaxed lime

1 heaped teaspoon pul biber chile flakes

2 garlic cloves, crushed

Maldon sea salt flakes and freshly ground black pepper

SERVES 4 TO 6

First make the spiced butter. Put all the ingredients into a mixing bowl and season well with salt and pepper, then beat together with a wooden spoon. Lay out a sheet of plastic wrap and spoon the butter into the center. Seal the butter in plastic wrap and form it into a log shape, twisting the ends closed to tighten and seal the butter inside (like a candy in a wrapper). Refrigerate until needed.

Preheat the oven to 425°F. Line a baking pan with nonstick parchment paper. Place the halved potatoes cut-side up in the prepared baking pan. Drizzle generously with olive oil and season well with salt and pepper. Roast for 35 minutes, or until cooked through and nicely browned.

Remove the spiced butter from the refrigerator and cut it into small cubes. Scatter these over the potatoes, then roast for a further 5 minutes, until the butter has melted. Remove from oven, toss the potatoes to coat them well in the melted butter, and serve immediately.

SPICED POTATO RÖSTI

There are few things in life better than fried potatoes, and I like to take them to the next level by adding a little spice. Serving yogurt flavored with my Sabzi Sauce and a poached egg on the side transforms this into a spectacular side or main dish.

2¼lb new potatoes (or any waxy potato), unpeeled and coarsely grated

1 teaspoon cumin seeds

1 teaspoon black mustard seeds

1 teaspoon coriander seeds

1 teaspoon dried red chile flakes

1 teaspoon garlic granules

1 small pack (about 1oz) of dill, finely chopped

3 to 4 tablespoons ghee

2 tablespoons Sabzi Sauce (*see* page 195)

½ cup Greek yogurt

Maldon sea salt flakes and freshly ground black pepper

For the eggs (optional)
olive oil, for greasing

4 eggs

SERVES 2 TO 4

Put the grated potato into a large mixing bowl and season well with salt (be very generous, because this will be extracted later). Mix well and set aside for 10 minutes.

Once the salting time has elapsed, stir the potato again, then tip it out of the bowl onto a piece of cheesecloth or a clean dishcloth, or into a sieve, and squeeze the excess moisture from the potato. Put the potato into a clean bowl, add the spices, garlic granules, and dill and season generously with black pepper. Mix well with a fork until all the ingredients are evenly combined (avoid mixing with your hands, as you run the risk of releasing more moisture from the potato).

Heat a large, nonstick skillet, about 10½ inches in diameter, over medium-low heat. Add the ghee to the pan, and once hot, scatter the potato mixture evenly into the pan. Using a spatula, flatten and smooth the surface of the mixture, pressing down gently. Cook for 8 minutes, then carefully check to see if the underside has turned a deep golden brown; continue cooking for a further 2 minutes if necessary. Once the underside has turned golden brown, carefully flip the rösti over and cook the other side for 8 minutes. If you're worried about turning it over without breaking it, my tip is to hold a plate firmly against the skillet, quickly flip the whole thing onto the plate, then slide the rösti back into the pan to cook the other side.

If serving with poached eggs, bring a saucepan of water to a simmer. Line 4 small bowls or tea cups with plastic wrap leaving plenty of overhang, rub the plastic wrap with a little olive oil, and crack an egg into each. Gather up the plastic wrap around each raw egg, expelling any air, and twist it to seal. Tie each egg parcel closed with some kitchen string. Lower the egg parcels into the pan of boiling water and poach for 2 to 5 minutes, or until cooked to your liking. Use a slotted spoon to remove the parcels from the water.

Mix the Sabzi Sauce together with the yogurt. Serve with the rösti with the green yogurt and the poached eggs (if using).

"SHAKEN" SWEET QUICK-PICKLED ONIONS

I'm completely addicted to these onions and make them quite often, especially since they are ridiculously easy to prepare. Pile into a grilled cheese sandwich, toss into salads, or serve with curries, stews, and soups.

1 large red onion, halved and very thinly
    sliced into half-moons
1 tablespoon superfine sugar
1 tablespoon rice vinegar
1 teaspoon pul biber chile flakes
generous amount of Maldon sea salt
    flakes

MAKES A SMALL BOWLFUL

Combine all the ingredients in a lidded plastic container. Close the lid tightly and shake vigorously for a couple of minutes until the onion slices soften, then serve. Keep refrigerated for up to 2 days in a sealed container.

SMACKED CUCUMBER SALAD

Cucumbers are a much-loved Persian staple and we eat them by the pound. I wrote this recipe to appease my mother and her mad love for all things cucumber. It features regularly in our house because it's so easy to make and such a great accompaniment to many dishes.

1 tablespoon sesame seeds
1 large cucumber, bashed all over against
    a hard surface or with a rolling pin,
    then cut into batons or chunks
Maldon sea salt flakes

For the dressing
1 teaspoon coriander seeds
1 teaspoon sesame oil
1 tablespoon rose harissa
2 tablespoons honey
1 tablespoon rice vinegar
1 garlic clove, crushed
1 teaspoon nigella seeds
squeeze of lemon juice

SERVES 2 TO 4

Toast the sesame seeds in a dry skillet over medium-low heat for 4 to 5 minutes until browned, then remove from the heat and transfer to a bowl.

Put the coriander seeds for the dressing into the same pan and toast for about 1 minute, until they release their aroma. Remove from the heat, transfer to a mortar and pestle, and crush them lightly, grinding just enough to crack the seeds.

To make the dressing, mix the sesame oil, harissa, honey, vinegar, and garlic in a small bowl. Add the crushed coriander seeds, the nigella seeds, and the lemon juice and mix well.

Place the cucumber in a serving bowl, pour the dressing over them, season with salt, and, lastly, sprinkle with the toasted sesame seeds. Stir and serve.

SABZI SAUCE

Sabzi, the Persian word for herbs, is derived from the Persian word sabz, meaning green. This great little herby sauce is so versatile. Stir it into yogurt, use it to marinate halloumi, paneer, or feta, or as a salad dressing, or dollop it onto soups or into stews, or smear it onto toasted flatbreads and top with feta cheese and red chile flakes for a snack. You get the drift—you can use it in everything!

1 cup coarsely chopped flat leaf-parsley

1 cup coarsely chopped dill

½ cup coarsely snipped chives

1 cup coarsely chopped cilantro

1 long red chile, seeded if preferred

2 preserved lemons

1 tablespoon ground cumin

1 tablespoon ground coriander

1 fat garlic clove, crushed

1 cup olive oil

Maldon sea salt flakes and freshly
    ground black pepper

MAKES 1 JAR

Using a food processor or blender, blitz all the ingredients until the mixture is smooth.

Transfer the mixture to an airtight food container or, for a longer life, a sterilized jar, and store in the refrigerator for up to 1 week. The color may fade the longer you keep it, but this will not affect the taste.

SWEET TREATS

BEET HALVA TART

WITH PISTACHIO NUTS

This is my take on the classic Indian dessert of gajar ka halwa, a painstakingly slowly cooked dessert made with grated carrots, spices, ghee, and milk. I once tried something similar but with beets, which is how I came up with this version. It isn't as sweet as the Indian version because I prefer to let the natural flavors of the beets do the talking.

For the filling

½ cup unsalted butter

2 teaspoons ground cinnamon

seeds from 8 cardamom pods, finely ground using a mortar and pestle

2¼lb raw beets, peeled and grated

1 cup superfine sugar

1¼ cups milk

¼ cup pistachio nuts, coarsely chopped

For the pastry

2 cups all-purpose flour, plus extra for dusting

½ cup unsalted butter, softened

pinch of Maldon sea salt flakes

2 tablespoons superfine sugar

1 egg, beaten

1 egg yolk

SERVES 8 TO 10

First make the filling. Melt the butter in a large saucepan over medium heat, then add the spices. Stir for 30 seconds, then add the grated beets and sugar and mix well. Cook for about 5 minutes, or until the beets are soft. Pour in the milk and stir well, then lower the heat and let simmer for 30 to 45 minutes, stirring occasionally to prevent burning, until all the liquid has been absorbed by the beets. This process does take time, so be patient. Once all the liquid has been absorbed, let the mixture cool, then refrigerate it for at least 1 hour.

Next make the pastry. Put the flour, butter, salt, and sugar into a bowl and rub everything together with your fingertips, lifting the flour upward from the bottom of the bowl, until the mixture resembles sand. Then make a well in the center, add the egg and egg yolk, and incorporate them into the flour mixture to form a smooth ball of dough.

Select a tart pan with a diameter of 9½ inches. Tear a large square of plastic wrap and place it on your work surface. Dust generously with flour, then set the pastry dough on top, dust that with flour, and cover it loosely with another layer of plastic wrap. Using a rolling pin, roll out the dough until it is slightly larger than your pan. Remove the top layer of plastic wrap and carefully transfer the dough into the pan, discarding the lower layer of plastic wrap. Push the dough gently into the edges of the pan, leaving a little overhanging. Now sweep the rolling pin across the top of the pan to cut off the overhanging dough. Cover the tart shell with plastic wrap and refrigerate for at least 30 minutes (or overnight).

Preheat the oven to 350°F.

Remove the tart shell and the beet mixture from the refrigerator. Pour the beet mixture into the chilled tart shell. If you have one, transfer the pan onto a pizza stone, then bake for 40 to 45 minutes, or until the crust is crisp. Scatter the pistachios on top and gently press them into the filling. Leave the tart in the pan to cool completely before serving.

CINNAMON PAVLOVA
WITH SWEET LABNEH CREAM

Meringues are ideal after a heavy meal because they feel a lot lighter and more digestible than many other desserts (or so I keep telling myself!). I use sweetened labneh and cream, which really changes the character of a classic pavlova to something a bit different. The cinnamon meringue works beautifully with the figs, and Greek basil adds a refreshing touch.

For the meringue

6 large egg whites

1¼ cups superfine sugar

1 heaped teaspoon ground cinnamon

1 tablespoon cornstarch

1 teaspoon red wine vinegar

For the topping

2½ cups heavy cream

2 teaspoons vanilla bean paste

½ cup labneh

6 fat black figs, quartered

½ cup pistachio nut slivers (or coarsely chopped whole nuts)

2 to 3 tablespoons honey

handful of Greek basil

handful of mint, leaves picked, rolled up tightly, and thinly sliced into ribbons

SERVES 8 TO 10

Preheat the oven to 320°F. Select the largest baking sheet you have. Line it with nonstick parchment paper, then draw a circle 9½ inches in diameter in the center of the paper. Turn the paper over and you should still be able to see the circle, which you can use as a guide.

Using an electric hand mixer, beat the egg whites in a large mixing bowl until stiff peaks form, then slowly add the sugar, 1 tablespoon at a time, until it is all incorporated into the egg white. Add the cinnamon, cornstarch, and vinegar and continue to whip until they are well incorporated and the mixture is shiny and dense.

Fill the circle on the prepared baking sheet with the meringue mixture, then use a spatula to create peaks around the sides.

Transfer the baking sheet to the oven. Immediately reduce the temperature to 300°F and bake for 1½ hours, or until the meringue is cooked and crisp on the outside. Remove from the oven and let cool completely.

Make the topping when you are ready to serve. Using an electric hand mixer, whip the cream with the vanilla bean paste in a large mixing bowl until stiff peaks form. Once the cream is nice and firm but not overbeaten, gently fold in the labneh.

Spread the whipped cream over the top of the meringue, then arrange the figs on top. Scatter with the pistachios, drizzle with the honey, then scatter with the basil leaves and mint. Serve immediately.

SPICED CHEWY CHOCOLATE COOKIES

I'm fussy about cookies. They need to have the right texture: usually a little crunch on the outside and a lovely chewiness on the inside. Chocolate is a must and nuts are perfectly acceptable. These don't exactly qualify as normal cookies as they are more of a meringue, being soft, chewy, sticky, and so very addictive.

4 eggs whites

2½ cups confectioners' sugar, sifted

½ cup unsweetened cocoa powder, sifted

good pinch of salt

1 cup dark chocolate chips

3 teaspoons instant espresso, dissolved in 3 teaspoons warm water

2 teaspoons vanilla bean paste

2 teaspoons ground cinnamon

½ teaspoon chili powder

2 tablespoons butter, melted

MAKES 20

Preheat the oven to 350°F. Line your largest cookie sheet with nonstick parchment paper.

Using an electric hand mixer, whisk the egg whites in a large mixing bowl until stiff peaks form.

In a separate bowl, mix the confectioners' sugar, cocoa, and salt together, then stir in the chocolate chips. Use a spatula to carefully fold in the beaten egg whites, coffee, vanilla bean paste, and spices, ensuring you are folding rather than beating to incorporate air and prevent the mixture from flattening.

As soon as you've mixed the ingredients together, brush the nonstick parchment paper on the cookie sheet with the melted butter (this will make it easier to remove the baked cookies). Take heaped teaspoons of the mixture and dollop it onto the cookie sheet, leaving a gap of 1 inch between each cookie (they will spread during baking). Don't be tempted to use more than a heaped teaspoon of mixture, otherwise it will become impossible to remove each cookie in one piece once baked.

Bake for 12 minutes. The cookies will be soft when you remove them from the oven, but will crisp up as they cool. Leave them on the paper to cool. Then, using a metal spatula, carefully remove them from the paper. This job is slightly fiddly, so be gentle when lifting them off and your patience will be rewarded. Serve immediately.

ZUCCHINI, ORANGE & ALMOND CAKE
WITH SWEET YOGURT FROSTING

I am rather obsessed with finding ways to pack vegetables into cakes. I would stop short at onions, but I do love making cakes with parsnips, butternut squash, beets, and sweet potato. So, why not zucchini? Their water content helps keeps the cake nice and moist, and they pair very well with the ground almonds in this cake, which also happens to be gluten free. I just love the fragrant spike of orange zest in both the cake and the yogurt frosting.

3 large eggs

⅔ cup superfine sugar

finely grated zest of 3 unwaxed oranges

1½ cups ground almonds

2 large zucchini (about 10½oz in total), coarsely grated

⅔ cup salted butter, melted

For the frosting

⅔ cup thick Greek yogurt

½ cup confectioners' sugar, sifted

finely grated zest of 1 unwaxed orange, plus extra to decorate

SERVES 10

Preheat the oven to 350°F. Line a 9-inch springform cake pan with nonstick parchment paper.

Put the eggs and sugar into a large mixing bowl and beat together until pale and creamy. Then add the orange zest, ground almonds, zucchini, and, lastly, the melted butter. Beat until the batter is smooth.

Pour the batter into the prepared pan. Bake for 1 hour and 20 minutes, then remove from the oven and let cool in the pan.

To make the frosting, combine the ingredients in a small bowl.

Carefully remove the cake from the pan and set it on a serving plate. Spread the frosting over the top surface of the cake and sprinkle with extra orange zest. The cake will keep for 2 to 3 days in the refrigerator, but bring to room temperature before serving.

MANGO, BLACK PEPPER & CARDAMOM POLENTA CAKE

Mangoes are among my most favorite fruits in the whole wide world. I always look forward to the brief windows in which the different varieties are in season, from Thai and Indian to Pakistani and Brazilian. Between those times canned mango purée comes into its own. It really is a gift from the heavens. It's great for cocktails, sorbets, and, in this instance, slices of baked polenta. A little taste of something sweet yet spicy, this is ideal topped with cooling lime-spiked yogurt.

3 large eggs

⅓ cup superfine sugar

1 tablespoon vanilla bean paste

seeds from 6 cardamom pods, finely ground using a mortar and pestle

1 teaspoon freshly ground black pepper (grind it coarsely)

2⅔ cups best-quality polenta (not quick-cook)

⅔ cup butter, melted

30oz can sweetened mango pulp (purée)

For the lime yogurt

1 cup Greek yogurt

2 tablespoons confectioners' sugar

finely grated zest of 1 unwaxed lime

1 teaspoon vanilla bean paste

SERVES 10 TO 12

Preheat the oven to 350°F. Line a 14 x 10-inch baking pan or ovenproof dish with nonstick parchment paper.

Put the eggs, sugar, vanilla bean paste, ground cardamom, and pepper into a large mixing bowl and beat together. Once blended, add the polenta and melted butter and mix well, then stir in the mango purée.

Pour the batter into the prepared baking pan and tap the pan on the counter a few times to distribute it evenly and smooth out the surface. Bake for 40 to 45 minutes, until firm. Let the cake cool completely in the pan.

Stir all the ingredients for the lime yogurt in a bowl to combine.

You can either top the entire cake with the lime yogurt, or serve the yogurt on the side. Cut the cake into 10 to 12 slices to serve.

DARK CHOCOLATE & CHERRY SHEET BAKE

Sometimes you need a cake big enough to feed a crowd or to help you manage a few days' worth of stress when you clearly need a little therapy in sugary, spongy form. This is the cake for you. The cherries are frozen, so it's cheaper than using fresh cherries and means you can make the cake all year round. I suggest that, providing nobody is watching, you cut yourself a slab, lock yourself away, and devour it alone.

3½ cups frozen pitted cherries
    (no need to defrost)

6 large eggs

1⅓ cups superfine sugar

2 teaspoons vanilla extract

2 teaspoons ground cinnamon

3¼ cups all-purpose flour

1⅓ cups unsalted butter, melted

2 teaspoons baking powder

7oz dark chocolate chunks

⅓ cup milk

SERVES 12 TO 14

Remove the cherries from the freezer. Preheat the oven to 350°F. Line a 14 x 10 x 2-inch rectangular cake pan or ovenproof dish with nonstick parchment paper.

Put the eggs and sugar into a large mixing bowl and beat together until smooth. Then beat in the vanilla extract, cinnamon, flour, melted butter, and baking powder. Next, fold in the cherries and chocolate chunks, then stir in the milk to loosen the batter a little. Stir until evenly combined.

Pour the batter into the prepared cake pan or baking dish and bake for 45 minutes, or until a skewer or knife inserted into the center comes out clean. Let cool in the pan before slicing into squares to serve.

RAS EL HANOUT & BUTTERMILK SWEET LOAF CAKE

WITH ROSE ICING

Ras el hanout is a highly prized blend of spices that packs an earthy punch, so you wouldn't be terribly out of line for questioning my state of mind when I first made this cake. I am pleased to report that it was a winner and, by the way, it is the rose icing that really makes the cake by complementing the spiciness so beautifully.

3 eggs

¾ cup superfine sugar

1 teaspoon vanilla extract

1½ cups all-purpose flour

⅔ cup unsalted butter, melted

1 teaspoon baking powder

1 heaped tablespoon ras el hanout

⅔ cup buttermilk

For the topping

⅔ cup confectioners' sugar, sifted

3 teaspoons rosewater

few dried edible rose petals, to decorate
(optional)

SERVES 8

Preheat the oven to 350°F. Line a 2lb loaf pan with nonstick parchment paper.

Put the eggs and sugar into a large mixing bowl and beat together until smooth. Then beat in the vanilla extract, all-purpose flour, melted butter, baking powder, and ras el hanout and mix until smooth. Lastly, add the buttermilk and incorporate well.

Pour the batter into the prepared loaf pan and bake for 50 to 55 minutes, or until cooked through and a skewer or knife inserted into the center of the cake comes out clean. Let cool in the pan.

To make the icing, mix the confectioners' sugar and rosewater together in a small bowl until smooth. Once the cake has cooled, smooth the icing over the top. Sprinkle with the dried rose petals to decorate, if desired.

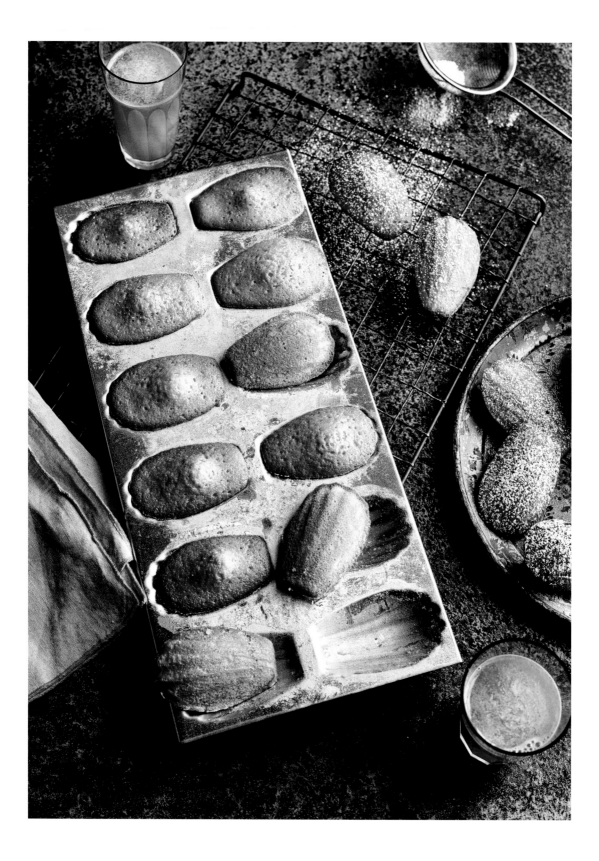

ORANGE, ALMOND & CARDAMOM MADELEINES

Madeleines are one of the great joys in my life and I love creating new variations. They're quick to make and small enough not to ruin a great meal, and if you are able to have them straight from the oven, they are really spectacular. I especially like madeleines spiked with a little lemon zest, but here I combine orange zest with cardamom for a lovely, gently spiced flavour. These make great gifts, that is, if you can bring yourself to give them away.

2 eggs

⅓ cup superfine sugar

2 teaspoons honey

seeds from 4 fat cardamom pods, finely
    ground using a mortar and pestle

finely grated zest of 2 unwaxed oranges

¼ cup unsalted butter, melted, plus
    extra for greasing

¾ cup all-purpose flour, plus extra
    for dusting

1 cup ground almonds

good pinch of fine sea salt

½ teaspoon baking powder

2 tablespoons milk

confectioners' sugar, for dusting
    (optional)

MAKES 14 TO 16

Put the eggs and sugar into a large mixing bowl and beat together until pale and creamy. Add the honey, ground cardamom, and orange zest and mix well. Now incorporate the melted butter, followed by the flour, ground almonds, salt, and baking powder. Mix until evenly combined, then stir in the milk. Cover the bowl with plastic wrap and refrigerate for 1 hour (or overnight, if you wish).

Preheat the oven to 400°F. Melt a little butter and, using a pastry brush, brush the recesses of a madeleine mold generously with the melted butter, then dust with a little flour, shaking off any excess.

Transfer 1 tablespoon (not too heaped) of the batter into each of the molds. Bake for 10 to 12 minutes, until nicely golden brown. Once cool enough to touch, remove from the molds. Repeat with any remaining batter. Dust the madeleines with a little confectioners' sugar, if desired, and serve immediately.

RASPBERRY & MASCARPONE NO-BAKE CHEESECAKE

I love cheesecake, but somewhere between all the complex versions out there, I lost my appetite for making it. However, this one is slightly different. It doesn't require baking or gelatin, and doesn't set in the same way as a regular cheesecake, so the texture is softer and creamier. Even if, like me, you are not the world's most talented pastry chef, it will still be a showstopper. This cheesecake is best made and refrigerated the day before you want to serve it.

9oz graham crackers

½ cup unsalted butter, melted

2⅔ cups full-fat cream cheese

1 cup mascarpone cheese

2¾ cups confectioners' sugar, sifted

3⅓ cups raspberries

1¼ cups pomegranate seeds

SERVES 8 TO 10

Line a 9-inch springform cake pan with nonstick parchment paper.

Place the graham crackers in a food bag and crush with a rolling pin until finely ground, or blitz in a food processor. Transfer the crumbs to a large mixing bowl, add the melted butter, and stir to combine. Tip the mixture into the lined baking pan and use a spatula to flatten it out into a smooth, even layer. Refrigerate for 1 hour.

Beat the cream cheese, mascarpone, and confectioners' sugar together briefly in a large mixing bowl until just combined, then add the raspberries and continue to stir until evenly mixed. The mixture becomes just a little thicker once the raspberries are stirred in, and their added moisture will not make the mixture too runny. Refrigerate for 1 hour.

Remove the cheesecake crust and the cream cheese mixture from the refrigerator and carefully spoon the cream cheese mixture onto the crust to fill the pan. Use a spatula to smooth out the surface until flat and even. Ensure the pomegranate seeds are dry, then scatter them on top of the cheesecake in a layer that covers the cream cheese mixture. Refrigerate for 8 hours, or overnight.

To remove the cheesecake from the cake pan, gently place it on a small overturned bowl, then unlatch and remove the sides of the pan. Carefully peel away the nonstick parchment paper and slide the cheesecake onto a large serving plate or platter. If the cheesecake has not set firmly enough for you to remove it cleanly from the pan, place it into the freezer for 20 minutes. Serve immediately.

SPICED CHOCOLATE, BLACK PEPPER & COFFEE MOUSSE

A well-made chocolate mousse has to be one of my favorite sweet treats. I love spiking chocolate with coffee; it's a wonderful flavor combination, and a little spice really does take this mousse to the next level. Serve them with thin, crisp wafers or coffee biscuits. The individual servings can be made a day or two in advance, so this really is the ideal dessert for entertaining.

5½oz dark chocolate (70 percent
    cocoa solids), broken into small
    chunks, divided
2 tablespoons unsalted butter
2 heaped teaspoons best-quality instant
    coffee or espresso granules
1 scant teaspoon ground cinnamon
seeds from 2 fat green cardamom pods,
    finely ground in a mortar and pestle
2 tablespoons boiling water
3 eggs, separated
¼ cup superfine sugar, divided
1 heaped teaspoon vanilla bean paste
½ cup heavy cream
freshly ground black pepper

MAKES 4 TO 6

Melt 3½oz of the chocolate in a small saucepan set over low heat. Remove the pan from heat and gently stir in the butter until the mixture has completely melted and is smooth. Set aside to cool.

Combine the coffee, cinnamon, and ground cardamom seeds in a small bowl with the boiling water and stir until the coffee granules dissolve. Let stand to cool.

Put the egg yolks and half the sugar into a large bowl and whisk together using an electric hand mixer until the mixture is pale. Add the cooled chocolate mixture, the cooled coffee and spice mixture, the vanilla bean paste, and a generous grinding of black pepper. In a separate mixing bowl, beat the egg whites until stiff peaks form. Set aside.

In another bowl, whip the cream together with the remaining sugar until stiff peaks form, but be careful not to overwork the mixture or it will become too thick. (To rescue overwhipped cream, add a little bit more cream and gently fold it in.)

Gently fold the egg whites into the chocolate mixture a heaped spoonful at a time, always folding rather than stirring, to keep the mousse light. Next, fold in the whipped cream gradually in the same way.

Divide the mixture between 4 glass dessert serving dishes or cups, or 6 espresso cups and let chill in the refrigerator for a minimum of 3 hours. Just before serving, finely chop the remaining chocolate chunks and scatter each serving to decorate.

BAKLAVA BUNS

I do love a cinnamon roll and these beauties are a hybrid of that classic fused with the Eastern staple baklava. These buns are comfortingly soft and doughy with a nutty crunch, and are the ultimate crowd-pleasers of any age. I have dispensed with the usual sweet baklava syrup and instead used honey to sweeten them. Add as much or as little as desired.

For the buns

3 cups strong bread flour, plus extra
    for dusting

¼oz envelope instant yeast

good pinch of fine sea salt

⅔ cup Greek yogurt

½ cup lukewarm water

2 to 3 tablespoons olive oil

For the filling

1 cup unsalted butter, softened

1 heaped teaspoon ground cinnamon

½ cup demerara (or turbinado) sugar

1½ cups chopped pistachio nuts

honey, to serve

MAKES 12

To make the buns, mix the flour, yeast, and salt together in a large mixing bowl, then add the yogurt, lukewarm water, and olive oil and mix to a dough. It should feel supple and soft, so if the dough seems sticky, add a little more flour. If it seems too dry, add a little extra olive oil to bring the dough together. Shape the dough into a ball, cover the bowl with a clean dishcloth, and let stand somewhere warm to rise for 1½ hours.

Preheat the oven to 400°F. Line 2 baking sheets with nonstick parchment paper.

Mix the butter with the cinnamon and set aside.

Dust a clean work surface with a little flour, then roll out the dough to a rectangular shape of about 10 x 20 inches. Spread the butter mixture across the surface of the dough, leaving a 1-inch border. Sprinkle the sugar evenly across the buttered surface, then scatter with the pistachios.

Curl up the long edge of dough closest to you and start to roll it up as tightly as possible away from yourself. When you have finished rolling the dough press it down to make it stick together. Using a very sharp knife, trim the ends, then carefully slice the dough into 12 equal disks. Place 6 slices on each prepared baking sheet, ensuring they are spaced well apart. For best results, bake one sheet of buns at a time for 18 to 20 minutes, or until golden brown.

Drizzle each bun with honey as desired and serve warm.

BABY BUTTERNUT BAKLAVA PIES

I love baklava in all its nut-filled, syrupy glory, but the truth is that many Westerners find more than one piece or two a bit too sweet. So when making Middle Eastern-style desserts to suit Western tastes, these little babies were born. The addition of butternut squash gives them a wonderful texture, and I have substituted confectioners' sugar for the syrup, which makes these the perfect sweet treat without sending you over the edge.

6 sheets of filo pastry, each cut into
    8 squares
confectioners' sugar, for dusting

For the filling
1¼ cups raw cashews
1⅔ cups ready-roasted chopped
    hazelnuts
finely grated zest of 1 unwaxed orange
⅔ cup unsalted butter, melted, plus
    extra for greasing, divided
2 teaspoons ground cinnamon, plus
    extra for dusting
10½oz butternut squash, peeled,
    seeded, and coarsely grated
2 tablespoons honey
3½ tablespoons superfine sugar

MAKES 12

Preheat the oven to 415°F. Spread the cashews across a baking pan and roast for 8 to 10 minutes, or until golden but not too dark brown. Let cool, then blitz the cashews in a food processor until finely chopped.

Put the chopped cashews into a large mixing bowl with the chopped hazelnuts, orange zest, half the melted butter, the cinnamon, butternut squash, honey, and superfine sugar and mix well until evenly combined.

Reduce the oven temperature to 400°F.

Grease a 12-hole muffin pan. Overlap 2 squares of filo pastry to resemble a star, then push the star into one of the holes in the prepared muffin pan. Repeat to line each of the remaining holes.

Divide the filling mixture equally between the pastry-lined holes. Press down on the filling with the back of a spoon to compress it, then flatten down the surfaces.

With the remaining filo pastry, take 2 squares, crumple them together in your hand, and place on top of one of the pie fillings. Brush with some of the remaining melted butter, then fold over the pastry edges to seal the pie. Brush the tops and edges with more melted butter. Repeat with the remaining pastry squares to seal all the pies. Bake for 25 minutes, or until golden brown.

Let the pies cool completely in the pan. When ready to serve, dust with a little confectioners' sugar and sprinkle with a little cinnamon.

SPICED APPLE, THYME & HAZELNUT CAKE
WITH CINNAMON CREAM

Apples are so plentiful, and their delicate sweetness is delicious in salads. In a cake, I feel apples need a nut element to enhance them. This thyme-scented cake can easily be made a day in advance, as the apple keeps it moist. The hazelnut element complements the apple beautifully and adds a lovely crunch.

3 large eggs

1 cup superfine sugar

2 teaspoons vanilla bean paste

1 tablespoon thyme leaves, finely chopped

1 heaped teaspoon ground cinnamon

1 teaspoon ground ginger

2 cups all-purpose flour

1 heaped teaspoon baking powder

1 cup unsalted butter, melted

¾ cup whole or halved blanched hazelnuts, lightly toasted in the oven (reserve a small handful to garnish)

2 apples, peeled, cored, and cut into ½-inch cubes

For the cinnamon cream

1¼ cups heavy cream

1 heaped teaspoon ground cinnamon

3 to 4 tablespoons confectioners' sugar, sifted

1 teaspoon vanilla bean paste

SERVES 8 TO 10

Preheat the oven to 350°F. Line a 9- or 9½-inch springform cake pan with nonstick parchment paper.

Beat together the eggs, sugar, vanilla bean paste, thyme, cinnamon, and ginger in a large mixing bowl to combine. Add the flour and baking powder and mix well, then beat in the melted butter until the batter is smooth. Stir in the hazelnuts, then carefully fold in the apple.

Pour the batter into the prepared cake pan and use a spatula to smooth over and flatten the surface. Now scatter the surface of the batter with the reserved hazelnuts. Bake for 1 hour and 10 minutes, or until golden brown on top. Remove the cake from oven and let cool in the pan.

To make the cinnamon cream, whip the ingredients together in a mixing bowl, using either a balloon whisk or an electric hand mixer, until the mixture is relatively stiff but still light and not overly dense. Serve the cake with a generous dollop of the cinnamon cream.

PISTACHIO, LEMON & RICOTTA CAKE

This cake is incredibly easy to make and really pleases a crowd. It tends to get eaten very quickly and for good reason; the ricotta gives it a moist texture, and the lemon and pistachio are a brilliant combination. The only way this cake could possibly be improved would be to add a nice cup of tea and some peace and quiet.

3 large eggs

1 cup superfine sugar

finely grated zest of 2 unwaxed lemons

2 teaspoons vanilla bean paste

2 cups all-purpose flour sifted with
    2 teaspoons baking powder

1 cup unsalted butter, melted

14oz ricotta cheese

1½ cups shelled pistachio nuts; 1 cup
    finely blitzed in a food processor
    and ½ cup kept whole

SERVES 10 TO 12

Preheat the oven to 350°F. Line a large, deep rectangular ovenproof dish or cake pan, about 15 x 10 x 3¼ inches in size, with nonstick parchment paper.

Put the eggs, sugar, lemon zest, vanilla bean paste, and ricotta into a large mixing bowl and beat together until evenly combined. Beat in the flour and baking powder mixture to incorporate, then beat in the melted butter Add the ground and whole pistachios and give everything a thoroughly good stir to ensure the batter is smooth and evenly combined.

Pour the batter into the prepared dish and use a spatula to ensure it is evenly distributed and that the surface is smooth and flat. Bake for 45 minutes, or until golden on top and a skewer or knife inserted into the center comes out clean. Let cool in the baking dish or cake pan, then cut into slices to serve.

INDEX

AUTHOR'S ACKNOWLEDGMENTS

To my agent and confidante, Martine Carter, who knows me better than I know myself, and to whom I owe everything… thanks for listening to more of my problems than any good agent should ever have to, and for guiding me through the jungle that is my career with patience, truth, and much kindness.

To my publisher and much-valued friend, Stephanie Jackson at Octopus Publishing who gave me my big break, puts up with my late submissions and strong-willed nature— thank you for always leading me through each project, and for your brutal honesty always letting me know exactly where I stand.

To Caroline Brown, publicity director at Octopus Publishing, and to your razor-sharp, brilliant team including Karen, Ellen, Matt & Meg who do so much hard graft to support every new book release—I am so grateful to you all for your support and guidance.

To my incredible photographer and much-loved friend, the brilliant, kind, and patient Kris Kirkham. You know you are my brother-from-another-mother, and please know, no matter where I am or what I am doing, I will always be ready to share a meal with you and will have a seat waiting for you at my table. You just "get me" and I don't even have to say anything, brother. Thanks for all your hard work, and to your assistant Eyder Rosso Goncalves, for his endless and much-appreciated cups of tea and coffee, and for always pretending to not be hungry and then eating six of everything I made.

I would like to extend a special thanks to my editor Sybella Stephens who translates "Sabrina garble talk" into normal English … my dear, you have the patience of a saint!

To Jonathan Christie, Jazzy 'Fizzle' Bahra, Peter Hunt, and Fran Johnson for designing and creating the most beautiful books and covers every time. You have my utmost sympathies for having to work with me, but God knows, I have so much respect for you all.

A big thank you to my food stylist Laura Field, and her assistants Hilary Lester, Sonali Shah, Lizzie Evans, and Sophie Pryn.

A big and very heartfelt thank you to Kevin Hawkins for all your inside wisdom and guidance whenever I've needed it, and to all the unsung heroes at Octopus Publishing. Although I rarely see you, and to those of you who I've not met, never a day goes by where I don't thank my lucky stars to have so many dedicated, hard-working people making my books the success that they are. I am incredibly fortunate to be working with you all.

A huge thank you to Alison Goff and Denise Bates at Octopus Publishing for always supporting me and making me feel more like family.

And last, but by no means least, to my friends and loved ones... those who I eat with, laugh with, cry with, and who test my recipes—your love and support has, and will, continue to be the fuel that fires my creativity and gives me the confidence to keep on doing what I do. Feasting with people is something I don't take lightly; to feast with me—no matter where—means we are family. I love each and every member of my family, whether we are related or not, you have all been kind to me and taught me something valuable that I will always keep close to my heart.

And before I forget (although you know full well I could never forget), to the inimitable Mama Ghayour—the best friend, Mother, and PA a girl could ask for... Thanks for always being so proud of me, no matter what... love you lots, Mugsy.

Sabrina Ghayour is an Iranian-born, self-taught home cook turned chef, cookery teacher, and food writer. She made her name hosting the hugely popular "Sabrina's Kitchen" supper club in London, specializing in Persian and Middle Eastern flavors, and went on to be named the *Observer's* Rising Star in Food. Her award-winning debut, *Persiana*, is a worldwide bestseller, and her follow-up cook books, *Sirocco,* and *Feasts,* have been instant bestsellers.

"The golden girl of Persian cookery" — *Observer*

www.sabrinaghayour.com

 @SabrinaGhayour

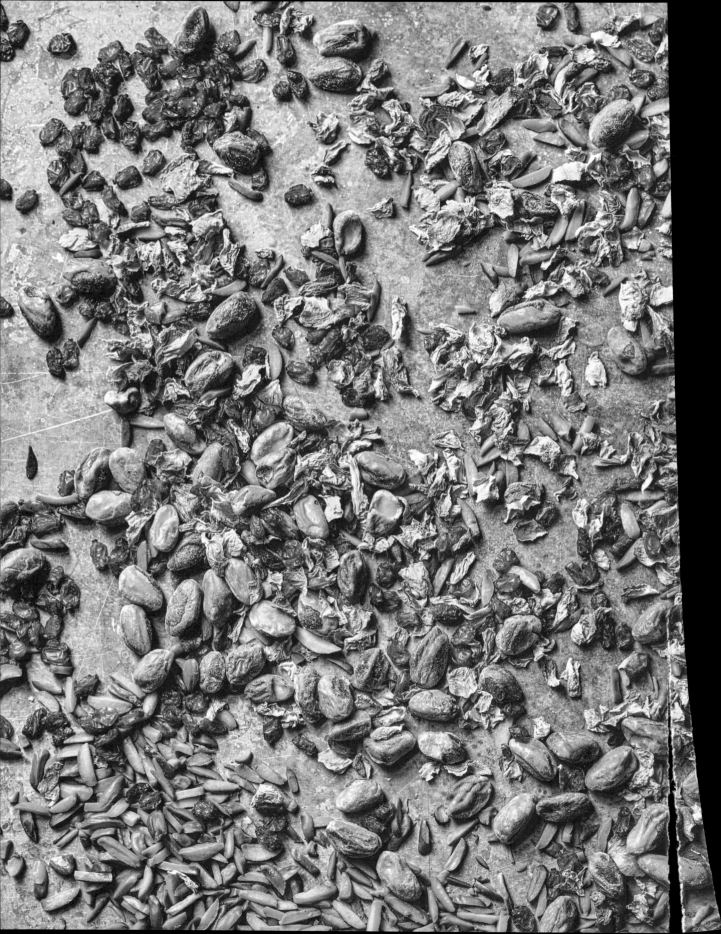